KU-268-961

THE WALES RUGBY MISCELLANY

THE

WALES RUGBY

MISCELLANY

BY ROB COLE & STUART FARMER

VSP

Vision Sports Publishing
2 Coombe Gardens,
London SW20 0QU

www.visionsp.co.uk

Published by Vision Sports Publishing. 2007

Text © Rob Cole and Stuart Farmer
Illustrations © Bob Bond Sporting Caricatures

ISBN 10: 1-905326-16-5
ISBN 13: 978-1-905326-16-7

All rights reserved. No part of this publication may be reproduced, stored in a retrieval system, or transmitted in any form or by any means, electronic, mechanical, photocopying, recording or otherwise, without the prior permission of the publishers.

This book is sold subject to the condition that it shall not, by way of trade or otherwise, be lent, re-sold, hired out, or otherwise circulated without the publisher's prior consent in any form of binding or cover other than that in which it is published and without a similar condition including this condition being imposed on the subsequent purchaser.

Printed and bound in the UK by
Cromwell Press Ltd, Trowbridge, Wiltshire

Typeset by Palimpsest Book Production Limited,
Grangemouth, Stirlingshire

A CIP catalogue record for this book is
available from the British Library

FSC Mixed Sources
Product group from well-managed forests and other controlled sources
www.fsc.org Cert no. TT-COC-2082
© 1996 Forest Stewardship Council

Vision Sports Publishing are proud that this book is made from paper certified by the Forest Stewardship Council

Foreword
By Gareth Edwards

Rugby is part of the DNA of Welshmen and women across the globe. It is at the heart of our very essence, defining us as individuals and as a nation. It has given me so much from boy through to man, and continues to provide me with great joy . . . and frequent frustration.

I can still remember the first time I picked up a ball as a youngster at Gwaun Cae Gurwen Primary School and will never forget the incredible privilege it was to win my first cap against France in Paris as a teenager 40 years ago.

I was lucky enough to win a further 52 caps and to make three tours with the British and Irish Lions. The game took me all over the world and, once I had retired, has provided me with a host of professional opportunities. Rugby has been good to me and I remain one of the game's biggest fans.

That's why it has been so nice to browse the fascinating facts, figures and stories gathered in this book by Rob Cole and Stuart Farmer. Many of the Gods of the game from my youth have found their way into the book. My early experiences of going to matches were of heading up the road to Stradey Park to see Llanelli play. I remember being mesmerised by the wizardry of scrum half Onllwyn Brace, of seeing the great Cardiff scrum half Lloyd Williams battling in blue and black against the Scarlets and of chasing autographs from the likes of Cyril Davies and Ray Williams. Little did I know then that one day my autograph would have some value to youngsters of future generations.

Those trips to Stradey Park, and later to international games at Cardiff Arms Park, used to inspire all the boys in the village to spend all their spare time playing with a rugby ball. It was always Wales against England and we would never finish until Wales had won. That was the law that could never be broken!

From GCG primary school I moved up to the secondary modern and then on to Pontardawe Technical School. That was where I first met up with Bill Samuel, who went on to have such a big influence on my career. Bill, as the master in charge of rugby, instilled the correct values in his pupils and helped me to reach a level that earned me a two year scholarship at Millfield School and a coveted Welsh Schools cap. Those formative years were vital in preparing me for a senior career with Cardiff, Wales and the Lions and I never forgot the lessons taught to me at school and by Bill.

My other great rugby education came when I joined Cardiff rugby club. Over the past 40 years the Arms Park has almost been my second home, for both club and country. I'll never forget my first international match at the ground. Having made my international debut in Paris we returned to Cardiff for the final Five Nations game against a Triple Crown chasing England. All of a sudden those battles in the back yard and school fields were becoming a reality. Wales had lost every game in the championship up to the point and the selectors reacted by picking a novice full back in Keith Jarrett. We won the game, Keith scored 19 points and the game became known as 'Jarrett's Match'.

That game is very special to me as it was also the last chance I got to play with my boyhood hero Dewi Bebb. I remember being at the Arms Park for my first international and watching Dewi, the great Swansea and Lions wing, scoring a try in the corner against England. It was my great pleasure to give him a scoring pass to score in his final game against the same opposition in 1967.

If Dewi was one of my heroes, then the exploits of many, many more have been unearthed in this book. I loved reading about Dai 'Tarw' Jones, the giant second row who remains the only Welsh player to have beaten New Zealand for Wales in both rugby union and rugby league. What a legend he must have been.

Then there are players like Arthur Gould, Billy and Jack Bancroft, Billy Trew, Claude Davey, Wilf Wooller, Bleddyn Williams and Dr Jack Matthews. They blazed the trail for so many of us to follow and their example remains an inspiration to current and future generations of Welsh players.

The moment you pull on the red jersey emblazoned with the three feathers to become a Welsh international is something that stays with you forever. Running out at the Arms Park, joining the crowd in singing the national anthem and, of course, beating England, is an indescribable feeling.

I've been fortunate enough to experience that and I know how lucky I have been. I hope that the endeavours, many record breaking, some amusing and others slightly tragic, recorded in this book will continue to inspire players, coaches, referees and fans long into the future.

William Webb Ellis may have been credited with picking up the ball for the first time and running with it at Rugby School. But I reckon he had dropped a perfectly good pass from a Welshman earlier in the move.

If Wales can't take the credit for founding the game of rugby union, then it has certainly played a huge part in its development. Long may that continue.

Gareth Edwards

Acknowledgements

We would to thank the team at Vision Sports Publishing, particularly Jim Drewett and Toby Trotman for their ideas, input and enthusiasm.

To that world great Gareth Edwards for kindly agreeing to pen the foreword, and to John Jenkins for his studious work at the National Library of Wales in verifying birth records of international rugby players.

Also a special mention for the efforts of John Kennedy and Terry Grandin at Westgate, who aided immeasurably in the creation and proofing of the manuscript.

As with all books of this type the odd omission and inaccuracy may appear. If any reader has any further information, which may be of use, would they please contact the author through the publishers?

Happy digging . . .

Rob Cole and Stuart Farmer

Authors' notes: The term 'international' refers to an international match in which a country awards caps. Occasionally we have used 'test match' to refer to the same criteria even though strictly speaking the term is an Australian one which has never been fully accepted in the UK.

Where appearances are marked thus (25+3) it means that a player has started 25 capped matches and been a replacement who had some game time in three further matches. Any caps gained for the British & Irish Lions or their forerunners are not included.

Any statistics pertaining to club representation take account only of the club that player was appearing for at the time of his cap, and not any other clubs he may have appeared for before or after the dates of his Wales career.

The stats in *The Wales Rugby Miscellany* are correct up until August 18th 2007.

— IN THE BEGINNING —

Whether you trace the roots of rugby back to the handball games played by the Romans at forts like Caerleon and Caerwent, the rough and tumble game of Normandy known a 'la soule', the Cornish game of 'hurling' dating back to the Bronze Age or the inter-village 'cnappan' battles found in Pembrokeshire in the 17th century, there is no denying the game of rugby is a vital ingredient in the lifeblood of the Welsh nations.

The game was introduced to Wales at Lampeter College in the mid-19th century using the Rugby School rules. In September 1875, the South Wales Football Club was created in Brecon "with the intention of playing matches with the principal clubs in the west of England and the neighbourhood – the Rugby rules will be the adopted code".

In 1878, a new body came into existence, the South Wales Football Union, which took over the regulation of competition and the selection of representative teams. But it was the selection of the first Welsh team by the remarkable Richard Mullock (see *Welsh Sport's Mr Fix It*, page 26) to face England at Mr Richardson's Field, Blackheath on 19th February 1881 that hastened the formation of what we now know as the Welsh Rugby Union.

Mullock negotiated a fixture with the RFU and picked the Welsh team himself. He arranged a trial match which never took place, and had to accept two changes of date for the match.

Some players refused to play, feeling it wasn't a truly representative Welsh team, two of his selections didn't turn up and Mullock was forced to invite two students who had gone to Blackheath to watch the game to play. It was a landslide on the pitch, with England running in 13 tries. In modern day scoring they would have topped 80 points.

Nevertheless, less than a month later a group of 11 clubs – Swansea, Lampeter, Llandeilo, Cardiff, Newport, Llanelli, Merthyr, Llandovery, Brecon, Pontypool and Bangor – came together at the Castle Hotel, Neath on 12th March 1881 to form the Welsh Rugby Football Union. It was a meeting that took place on the same day as Cardiff beat Llanelli in the fourth South Wales Challenge Cup final in Neath. The union has been the guardian of Wales' national sport ever since.

Cyril Chambers, of the Swansea Football Club, was elected the first President of the WRFU and Richard Mullock, of Newport, became the first Honorary Secretary and Treasurer.

— LIST OF FOES —

Here is the full list of Wales' opponents:

Opponent	First played	Pld	W	D	L
England	19th Feb 1881	116	51	12	53
Ireland	28th Jan 1882	112	61	6	45
Scotland	8th Jan 1883	112	61	3	48
New Zealand Natives	22nd Dec 1888	1	1	0	0
New Zealand	16th Dec 1905	23	3	0	20
South Africa	1st Dec 1906	19	1	1	17
France	2nd Mar 1908	83	42	3	38
Australia	12th Dec 1908	25	9	1	15
New Zealand Army	21st Apr 1919	1	0	0	1
Romania	12th Nov 1983	8	6	0	2
Fiji	9th Nov 1985	6	6	0	0
Tonga	12th Jun 1986	6	6	0	0
Samoa	14th Jun 1986	6	3	0	3
Canada	3rd Jun 1987	9	8	0	1
United States	7th Nov 1987	6	6	0	0
Namibia	2nd Jun 1990	3	3	0	0
Barbarians	6th Oct 1990	2	1	0	1
Argentina	9th Oct 1991	11	7	0	4
Zimbabwe	22nd May 1993	3	3	0	0
Japan	16th Oct 1993	6	6	0	0
Portugal	18th May 1994	1	1	0	0
Spain	21st May 1994	1	1	0	0
Italy	12th Oct 1994	14	11	1	2
Pacific Islanders	11th Nov 2006	1	1	0	0

Note: Covers the 576 internationals played by Wales between February 1881 and August 18th 2007.

— WELSH RUGBY FIRSTS —

The first Welsh international was held on 19th February 1881 against England on Mr Richardson's Field, Blackheath. Wales conceded 13 tries to lose by seven goals, six tries and one drop goal to nil – or 82–0 in modern scoring values.

The first captain of Wales was Cambridge University student James Alfred Bevan, who had been born in Australia.

The first Welsh victory came in their second match, which was at Lansdowne Road, Dublin against Ireland on 28th January 1882. Wales won by two goals and tries to nil.

The first Welsh try and points scorer was Newport's Tom Baker Jones. He scored after 26 minutes of the match against Ireland in Dublin in 1882.

The first Welshman to score with the boot was Llandovery College's Charles Lewis against Ireland in 1882.

The first home Welsh international was played at St Helen's, Swansea, on 16th December 1882 against England. Wales lost by two goals and four tries to nil.

The first Welsh player to score against England was the Oxford University student Charles Allen. He crossed for a try in a game played at Leeds in 1884 and won by England by one goal and two tries to one goal.

The first international match to be played on Cardiff Arms Park was against Ireland on 12th April 1884. Wales won by a drop goal and two tries to nil after providing two players to the Irish to make up their team.

The first drawn match involving Wales was at Hamilton Crescent, Glasgow on 10th January 1885, when Scotland and Wales drew 0–0.

The points system was used for the first time when Scotland played Wales at Cardiff Arms Park on 1st February 1890. Wales lost 1–5.

The first set of brothers to play for Wales were the Gwynns, David and William. David played six times for Wales between1882–91, making his debut against England. William won five caps between 1884–85.

The first set of brothers to play in the same Welsh XV were the Goulds, Bob and Arthur. They played together five times, the first against England on 3rd January 1885, before Arthur played in tandem with another brother, Bert, three times.

The first father and son to play for Wales were Tom Baker Jones (six caps, 1882–85) and Paul Jones (one cap, 1921).

The first Welsh player to score against Scotland was Tom Judson on 8th January 1883 at Raeburn Place, Edinburgh. Wales lost by three goals to one.

The first victory on Welsh soil was at Cardiff Arms Park on 12th April 1884, when Wales beat Ireland by two tries and one drop goal to nil.

The first drop goal scored by a Welsh player was by Buller Stadden at Cardiff Arms Park against Ireland in 1884.

The first schoolboy to play for Wales was William Thomas. He was capped against Scotland in 1885 at the age of 18 years, nine months, 19 days while still a pupil at Llandovery College.

Wales' first win on English soil came on 12th March 1887, when Wales beat Ireland at Birkenhead in what was deemed a 'home' game for Wales. The game was played in England to ease the expense of travelling for the Irish team, with Birkenhead close to the port of Liverpool.

William Thomas became the first Welsh player to tour Australia and New Zealand with a British team when he played 15 games on the 1888 tour.

The first game Wales played against a touring side was against the New Zealand Natives at St Helen's on 22nd December 1888. Wales won by 1 goal and 2 tries to nil.

— SPORTING PIONEERS —

Among the members of the South Wales Football Club's inaugural 'Match Committee' was Neath's Tom Whittington. The founding father of one of Wales' oldest clubs – the first recorded match in Wales was between Swansea and Neath on 7th February 1872 – he was also the first international player to play in a Welsh club side.

Although listed as 'Merchiston Castle', the Welsh-born doctor was playing for Neath when he made his one and only appearance for Scotland in a drawn 20-a-side match against England on 3rd March 1873. Whittington attended Merchiston Castle school and then studied medicine at Edinburgh University before returning to practice in his home town of Neath. A fine all-round sportsman, he also played cricket for Glamorganshire in the 1860s and 1870s.

His son, 'Tal', went on to score more than 4,500 runs for Glamorgan and toured with the MCC to the West Indies in 1910/11 and 1912/13. He helped to secure first-class status for the Welsh county and was both captain and then secretary of the club.

Another member of that early SWFC committee was the Swansea skipper, Charles Campbell Chambers. He went on to become the first President of the Welsh Rugby Football Union. He served in that post from March to September 1881 before handing over to the Earl of Jersey.

Chambers' brother, Eton and Trinity College, Cambridge educated John Chambers, was one off the founders of the Amateur Athletics Association in 1880 and its forerunner, the Amateur Athletic Club, in 1866.

The Earl of Jersey, meanwhile, combined his role as President of the WRU with that of President of the AAA.

— QUICK LEARNERS —

Neath hooker Barry Williams holds the record for the fastest debut try by a Welsh player. He took just two minutes to cross the French line in a friendly fixture in September 1996 that ended in 40–33 victory for France. The four players to score inside ten minutes of their debut are:

Mins	Player	Versus	Date
2	Barry Williams	v France (Cardiff)	25th September 1996
7	Gareth Cooper	v Italy (Rome)	8th April 2001
8	Carwyn Davies	v Samoa (Cardiff)	12th November 1988
8	Richard Rees	v Zimbabwe (Harare)	6th June 1998

— THE FIVE NATIONS BEGINS —

The launch season of the Five Nations Championship is generally accepted as 1910 when France played all of the Home Unions for the first time. Wales had claimed Grand Slams in 1908 and 1909 having met the French as well as England, Scotland and Ireland (see *Grand Slam Cheers*, page 16), but the other teams had not all played France. So the first game in Five Nations history took place on Saturday, 1st January, 1910, in front of only 4,000 spectators at Swansea's St Helen's ground.

Even the French thought they were going to be soundly beaten, their captain Gaston Lane declaring the night before the game he felt Wales would win by 35 points.

It didn't help that the French party had departed Paris with only 14 players when front row Helier Tilh pulled out because of military duties. French officials trawled Paris to try to find a replacement and eventually discovered Joe Anduran working in a picture gallery on Rue La Boetie.

He arrived in Swansea on the morning of the match and joined three Sporting Club Universitaire de France (SCUF) clubmates in the French pack. They were totally destroyed as Wales ran in ten tries in a 49–14 victory.

Among a cluster of records it was Wales' highest score against any team, their most tries in a championship match and Jack Bancroft's 19 points were an individual record. So were his eight conversions.

The points aggregate of 63 stood as the highest in an international match until South Africa beat France 38–25 in Bloemfontein in 1975. It was also Wales' 11th successive victory – a record that still stood in 2007.

— TAKE A BREAK —

Sam Ramsey became the first player to be capped from Treorchy when he won the first of his two caps against England at Blackheath on 4th January 1896. Wales lost 25–0 and Ramsey was dropped – for eight years.

He made his second appearance against England in a 14–14 draw at Leicester on 9th January 1904. The eight-year gap is the longest between caps of any Welsh player.

Cardiff hooker Geoff Beckingham had to wait five years to add a third cap to the two he won in the 1953 Five Nations championship. He won his second cap against Scotland on 7th February 1953 and was not selected again until 29th March 1958, when he played his final game against France.

— TAKING UP ARMS —

The traditional home of Welsh rugby, Cardiff Arms Park, was developed on what had been a stretch of the River Taff. In 1803, the Marquis of Bute handed over a "swampy meadow" behind the Cardiff Arms Hotel, sited in what is now Womanby Street.

The first sporting event staged on the ground was a cricket game organised by Cardiff Cricket Club in August 1848 against a Newport and Tredegar team that included players from Oxford, Clifton and Somerset. Cardiff won by 10 wickets over two innings.

Two years later the River Taff was re-routed 300 yards west so that land could be reclaimed to build the Great Western Railway and Cardiff Central Station. It wasn't until 1874 that the first recorded rugby match was played on the ground that took its name from the adjacent public house. On 21st November the Wanderers club met a Glamorgan 2nd XV. A local Cardiff newspaper report stated:

"Thirty and forty muscular young men met for a trial of skill and strength. Shins were barked in large numbers, the equilibrium of many was upset and, in short, there was war to the knife between the opposed parties.

"The match commenced early in the afternoon and was continued for several hours. The contest was very close and exciting and it was a difficult matter to decide which party was superior to the other.

"Two rogues were made by each, to which we may add a try on the part of Glamorgan. Ultimately the match was discontinued by consent and was considered a drawn one.

"Many persons witnessed the match, notwithstanding the thick fog which prevailed."

The first of the 227 (up to August 2007) full Welsh rugby internationals played at the venue was on 12th April 1884, when Wales met Ireland. There have also been four further Tests at the ground when used as a neutral venue during Rugby World Cup competitions:

Date	Result
30th Oct 1991	New Zealand 13 Scotland 6 (3rd place match)
16th Oct 1999	Argentina 33 Japan 12
4th Nov 1999	New Zealand 18 South Africa 22 (3rd place match)
6th Nov 1999	Australia 35 France 12 (Rugby World Cup final)

— GARETH THE GREAT —

Alfie: number one!

Gareth Thomas overtook Gareth Llewellyn's Wales cap record in Sydney on 26th May 2007. He captained the side that day and he also scored a try to extend his Welsh try record to 38.

Another Gareth, Edwards, became the first Welsh player to reach 50 caps when he played against England at Twickenham in 1978. He made 53 consecutive appearances before hanging up his boots.

The top appearance makers in Welsh rugby are:

No	Name	Career	Caps	St+Rep
1	Gareth Thomas	1995–2007	96	91+5
2	Gareth Llewellyn	1989–2004	92	82+10
3	Neil Jenkins	1991–2002	87	81+6
4	Colin Charvis	1996–2007	88	80+8
5	Ieuan Evans	1987–1998	72	72
6	Martyn Williams	1996–2007	71	61+10
7	Stephen Jones	1998–2007	62	55+7
8=	Garin Jenkins	1991–2002	59	52+7
8=	Rob Howley	1996–2002	59	58+1
10	JPR Williams	1969–1981	55	55
11	Robert Jones	1986–1995	54	53+1
12=	Gareth Edwards	1967–1978	53	53
12=	Scott Gibbs	1991–2001	53	53
12=	Dwayne Peel	2001–2007	54	35+19
15=	Scott Quinnell	1993–2002	52	50+2
15=	Mark Taylor	1994–2005	52	49+3
17	Dai Young	1987–2001	51	47+4

— IRELAND BORROW TWO FROM WALES —

Ireland's first matches against Wales were treated as an inconvenience by the men from the Emerald Isle, the Irishmen not considering Wales strong enough opponents.

The initial game at Lansdowne Road in 1882 was treated with such apathy by the Irish players that only four of the originally selected team actually turned out and Ireland duly paid the penalty losing by two goals, and two tries to nil.

A year later the attitude was little better with Ireland refusing to play Wales at all. And when Ireland visited the Arms Park on 12th April 1884, they once more had extreme difficulty in getting a truly representative team to make the journey. In fact, they were forced to borrow two Newport players to make up the numbers. There is much conjecture, and very little hard evidence, as to the identity of most of the Ireland side which took to the field that day. But noted Irish historians now believe that it contained Welshmen Charles Jordan and J. McDaniel. Jordan was the brother of Henry who won three caps between 1885 and 1889.

— WILKO LEADS THE WAY —

Jonny Wilkinson leads the way as the biggest Dragon slayer of them all with an average of 19 points per game in his seven matches against Wales.

Altogether, Wilko has amassed 137 points against the Welsh and has scored in every way. He is eight points clear of the Italian star Diego Dominguez, who scored 112 points in eight outings against Wales.

Name	Country	Apps	Tries	Cons	Pens	DGs	Pts
Jonny Wilkinson	England	7	1	24	24	4	137
Diego Dominguez	Italy	8	-	11	26	4	112
Percy Montgomery	South Africa	7	4	18	10	-	86
Matt Burke	Australia	5	2	13	16	-	84
David Humphreys	Ireland	6+3	-	12	18	2	84
Gavin Hastings	Scotland	9	1	5	21	-	77
Chris Paterson	Scotland	8+1	4	7	13	1	76
Felipe Contepomi	Argentina	7	3	7	14	1	74
Dan Carter	New Zealand	4	3	14	10	-	73
Grant Fox	New Zealand	4	-	24	7	-	69

— FAVOURITE DAY —

The most popular day for future Wales internationals to be born is 2nd March. Nine players have been born on that day, including two of the greatest full backs in the history of the game, Billy Bancroft and J.P.R. Williams.

Player	Born	Caps	Years played
Billy Bancroft	1871	33	1890–1901
Jack Jones	1886	14	1908–21
Dan Jones	1907	1	1927
Eddie Watkins	1916	8	1935–39
Ray Prosser	1927	22	1956–61
Ian Jones	1940	1	1968
J.P.R. Williams	1949	55	1969–81
Rob Ackerman	1961	22	1980–85
Richie Collins	1962	28	1987–95

— ANY DAY OF THE WEEK —

Although Saturday is by far the most common day of the week on which Wales have played, there have in fact been internationals played on every other day of the week.

MONDAY

Scotland v Wales, 8th January 1883: The first game between the two countries.

Wales v France, 25th March 1912: Billy Trew and Dicky Owen missed the match because they wanted to go on tour with Swansea to Devon.

TUESDAY

France v Wales, 28th February 1911: Played at Parc des Princes on Shrove Tuesday.

WEDNESDAY

Wales v France, 4th September 1991: First floodlit international at Cardiff Arms Park.

Wales v Argentina, 9th October 1991: Floodlit World Cup clash with the Pumas

THURSDAY

France v Wales, 23rd March 1922: Two players were dropped from the starting line-up just before kick-off because the selectors felt their replacements would be better suited to the hard-baked pitch at Stade Colombes.

France v Wales, 27th March 1924: Ossie Male was dropped from the team on the train en route to Paris.

FRIDAY

Wales v Japan, 26th November 2004: Wales' biggest home victory – 98–0.
Wales v Fiji, 11th November 2005: A narrow squeak in the Autumn Series.

Wales v Canada, 17th November 2006: Another Autumn Series Friday night game.

SUNDAY

Australia v Wales, Brisbane, 11th June 1978: First Sunday fixture for Wales.

Wales v Western Samoa, 6th October 1991: Wales' first home fixture in the Rugby World Cup.

Ireland v Wales, 3rd February 2002: Wales' first Sunday Six Nations fixture.

Wales v France, 7th March 2004: First home Sunday fixture in Six Nations.

— HOME FROM HOME . . . —

Wales have played 'home' fixtures at seven venues, although the current home of Welsh rugby has had three names. Prior to being called the Millennium Stadium, the venue was known as the National Ground and, most famously of all, Cardiff Arms Park.

Swansea's St Helen's ground hosted Wales' first home fixture against England on 16th December 1882, and Newport's Rodney Parade was next on the list in 1884. Cardiff Arms Park was used for the first time on 12th April 1884, and made a winning debut as Wales notched their first international win by a drop goal and two tries to nil over Ireland.

Llanelli's Stradey Park was the next home venue, although the first of five games taken to the west was actually played on an adjoining field to the rugby ground.

Two venues in England have been used to stage 'home' fixtures. Birkenhead Park near Liverpool was used in 1887 to cut down on travelling costs for the Irish, while Wembley Stadium hosted six matches in the 1990s as the nation awaited the Millennium Stadium.

Ground	**First used**	**Last match**	**Pld**	**W**	**D**	**L**
St Helen's, Swansea	16th Dec 1882	16th Nov 1997	51	33	1	17
Rodney Parade, Newport	12th Jan 1884	25th Mar 1912	6	4	0	2
Arms Park, Cardiff*	12th Apr 1884	17th Mar 2007	226	133	9	84
Stradey Park, Llanelli	8th Jan 1887	21st Nov 1998	5	4	1	0
Birkenhead Park	12th Mar 1887	12th Mar 1887	1	1	0	0
Racecourse, Wrexham	30th Aug 1997	27th Aug 2003	3	3	0	0
Wembley Stadium	29th Nov 1997	11th Apr 1999	6	2	0	4

* Millennium Stadium from 26th June 1999

— AND AWAY FROM HOME —

Wales were the first Test team to play at Twickenham on 15th January 1910, and the home of English rugby has been the most frequently visited ground by the Welsh side and its supporters.

But the ground at which Wales has enjoyed its biggest success is Lansdowne Road. Wales have an equal share of the spoils in Dublin with 17 wins and three draws in 37 fixtures.

Parc des Princes, on the other hand, was a graveyard of Welsh hopes with only three wins at the Paris venue in 15 visits.

Ground	First used	Last match	Pld	W	D	L
Twickenham, London	15th Jan 1910	6th Aug 2007	44	11	7	26
Murrayfield, Edinburgh	6th Feb 1926	10th Feb 2007	38	16	1	21
Lansdowne Road, Dublin	28th Jan 1882	26th Feb 2006	37	17	3	17
Stade Colombes, Paris	23rd Feb 1909	27th Mar 1971	20	11	1	8
Parc des Princes, Paris	28th Feb 1911	15th Feb 1997	15	3	0	12
Inverleith, Edinburgh	4th Mar 1899	2nd Feb 1924	11	4	1	6

— BIRD'S EYE VIEW —

Two Scottish fans got stuck on the top of the West Stand roof at Cardiff Arms Park the day before Wales were due to play Scotland on 7th February 1976. They had climbed up the ladder at the back of the stand by mistake and ended on the roof.

When they tried to get down the hatch had been closed and so they spent the night on one of the highest points in the Welsh capital. They were spotted just before kick-off the next day with their heads hanging over the edge of the roof. The key to their survival on what was one of the coldest nights of the year was half a bottle of scotch.

— BACK ROW BROTHERS —

Wales has fielded a club back row trio in ten internationals. The Llanelli trio of Emyr Lewis, Scott Quinnell and Mark Perego played together four times in the nineties and the Scarlets provided another two combinations.

Swansea provided the trio – Rob Appleyard, Stuart Davies and Colin Charivs – against France at Wembley in 1998.

The first club back row to play for Wales came from Newport. Brian Cresswell, Glyn Davidge and Geoff Whitson made history against Scotland on 6th February 1960 when they played in an 8–0 victory in Cardiff.

Here's the full list of Wales' one club International back rows:

6th Feb 1960 Wales 8, Scotland 0 Cardiff
Newport: Brian Cresswell, Glyn Davidge, Geoff Whitson

12th Mar 1960 Ireland 9, Wales 10 Dublin
Newport: Brian Cresswell, Glyn Davidge, Geoff Whitson

22nd May 1993 Zimbabwe 14, Wales 54 Bulawayo
Llanelli: Mark Perego, Emyr Lewis, Lyn Jones

10th Nov 1993 Wales 24, Canada 26 Cardiff
Llanelli: Scott Quinnell, Emyr Lewis, Lyn Jones

15th Jan 1994 Wales 29, Scotland 6 Cardiff
Llanelli: Emyr Lewis, Scott Quinnell, Mark Perego

5th Feb 1994 Ireland 15, Wales 17 Dublin
Llanelli: Emyr Lewis, Scott Quinnell, Mark Perego

19th Feb 1994 Wales 24, France 15 Cardiff
Llanelli: Emyr Lewis, Scott Quinnell, Mark Perego

19th Mar 1994 England 15, Wales 8 Twickenham
Llanelli: Emyr Lewis, Scott Quinnell, Mark Perego

21st May 1994 Spain 0, Wales 54 Madrid
Llanelli: Emyr Lewis, Scott Quinnell, Mark Perego

5th Apr 1998 Wales 0, France 51 Wembley
Swansea: Rob Appleyard, Stuart Davies, Colin Charvis

— WALES WORLD CUP CAPTAINS —

Year	Host nation		Captain
1987	New Zealand/ Australia	Richard Moriarty	Swansea
1991	England	Ieuan Evans	Llanelli
1995	South Africa	Mike Hall	Cardiff
1999	Wales	Robert Howley	Cardiff
2003	Australia	Colin Charvis	Unattached
2007	France	Gareth Thomas	Cardiff Blues

— THE WELSH FOREIGN LEGION —

Players born in 15 different countries have donned the Welsh shirt. England is not included in the list below because no fewer than 83 Welsh players capped between 18th February 1881 and 18th August 2007 were born there.

Argentina	John Morgan (2 caps, 1912–13)
Australia	James Bevan (1, 1881), Mapson Williams (1, 1923), Max Wiltshire (4, 1967–68), Gwilym Wilkins (1, 1994), Jason Jones-Hughes (3, 1999–2000), Brent Cockbain (23, 2003–07)
China	Dick Jones (1, 1929), Bobby Jones (3, 1926)
Egypt	Derrick Main (4, 1959), Graham Price (41, 1975–83)
Ireland	Frank Purdon (4, 1881–83)
W Germany	Paul Thorburn (36, 1985–91)
India	John Hinton (1, 1884), Tom Pearson (13, 1891–1903)
Kenya	Stuart Russell (1, 1987)
New Zealand	Hemi Taylor (24, 1994–96), Dale McIntosh (2, 1996–97), Shane Howarth (19, 1998–2000), Brett Sinkinson (20, 1999–2002), Matt Cardey (1, 2000), Sonny Parker (21, 2002–06)
Scotland	James Bridie (1, 1882), Dick Kedzlie (2, 1888), Sam Ramsey (2, 1896–1904), Tom Dobson (4, 1898–99)
Singapore	Clive Rees (13, 1974–83)
South Africa	Mickey Davies (2, 1939), Ian Jones (1, 1968), Hal Luscombe (16, 2003–07), Rhys Thomas (2, 2006–07), Ian Evans (5, 2006–07)
Zambia	Dafydd James (47, 1996–2007)
Zimbabwe	Andy Marinos (8, 2002–03)

— GRAND SLAM CHEERS —

The 1908 Grand Slam Team

Wales were the first nation to complete the Grand Slam – victories over England, Scotland, Ireland and France in one season – in 1908, although it was not recognised as a championship clean sweep. They repeated the feat in 1909, although in both those seasons there was not a full set of matches between the French and the home unions. England played France in 1908 and 1909, while Ireland met the French in 1909. Scotland didn't play them until 1910, which is considered to be the first official Five Nations Championship season.

While Wales are widely recognised as having completed the Slam in 1908 and 1909, the men in red can still lay claim to the first 'official' Five Nations Championship clean sweep in 1911. There was a 39-year gap before the next Grand Slam, in 1950, and another in 1952. The seventies saw further successes in 1971, 1976 and 1978 before the 'Class of 2005' secured the first Welsh Six Nations Grand Slam.

The games that sealed Welsh Grand Slam success:

Date	Opponent (Venue)	Result	Captain
14th Mar 1908	v Ireland (Balmoral, Belfast)	Won 11–5	Bert Winfield
13th Mar 1909	v Ireland (St Helen's)	Won 18–5	Billy Trew
11th Mar 1911	v Ireland (Cardiff)	Won 16–0	Billy Trew
25th Mar 1950	v France (Cardiff)	Won 21–0	John Gwilliam

22nd Mar 1952	v France (St Helen's)	Won 9–5	John Gwilliam
27th Mar 1971	v France (Paris)	Won 9–5	John Dawes
6th Mar 1976	v France (Cardiff)	Won 19–13	Mervyn Davies
18th Mar 1978	v France (Cardiff)	Won 16–7	Phil Bennett
19th Mar 2005	v Ireland (Cardiff)	Won 32–20	Michael Owen

— GRAND SLAM TEARS —

Welsh hopes were high of adding to their Grand Slam tally on three further occasions. In 1965 and 1988, Wales had already earned a Triple Crown, only to fall at the final hurdle, whilst they went to Twickenham in 1994 with the Grand Slam, Triple Crown and Championship at stake. They left with the Five Nations title only after losing 15–8 to England.

Date	Opponent (Venue)	Result	Captain
27th Mar 1965	v France (Paris)	Lost 13–22	Clive Rowlands
19th Mar 1988	v France (Cardiff)	Lost 9–10	Bleddyn Bowen
19th Mar 1994	v England (Twickenham)	Lost 8–15	Ieuan Evans

— THE MAGIC OF NO 10, NO 6 OR LETTER 'F' —

The first international to have numbered jerseys was the 1905 game in Cardiff between Wales and New Zealand. It wasn't until 1922, when England travelled to Cardiff, that both teams wore numbers in a Five Nations match.

The Scots were the last team to adopt numbering and by the 1930s it was commonplace for teams to be numbered in big matches. The way they were numbered, however, was a bit of a lottery. Wales refused to use No 13 for a period of years – they numbered 1-16 – and some teams started with their full back as No 1 and others No 15.

In the 1930s, Wales changed from numbers to letters. They wore letters against Scotland at Murrayfield in 1932. That practice lasted until 1950s. The great Welsh outside half of the thirties, Cliff Jones, wore the letter F on his back, while the legendary Cliff Morgan was No 6 in the 1950s. By the time the Welsh outside half factory had churned out David Watkins, Barry John and Phil Bennett they were wearing No 10.

— A HELL OF A GAME —

In 1941, a German parachute mine caused huge damage when it landed on Cardiff Arms Park. The great overhanging roof of the North Stand, opened only seven years earlier, was shattered and the rest of the stand was ruined. Parts of the South Stand and West Terrace were also wrecked and the WRU were in debt to the tune of £40,700 as a result of lost revenue.

The War Damage Commission finally agreed to pay for the damage and the North Stand was brought back into play on 5th March 1949. The Union finally cleared the debt in 1952.

When the American senator, Quentin Reynolds, visited the damaged ground soon after the mine had dropped he asked what the last game played at the ground had been. When he was told it was Wales v England a few years earlier, he commented: "It must have been one hell of a game!"

— TWICKENHAM OPENS —

Bridgend forward Ben Gronow had the honour of making the first play at Twickenham when Wales met England in the first international played there on 15th January 1910. He kicked off the game and then found himself doing exactly the same thing a minute later after England had scored the first try at their new home before another Welsh player had touched the ball.

Gronow had made his debut in the record breaking 49–14 win over France two weeks earlier as Wales made it eight championship wins in a row. But after England skipper Adrian Stoop had gathered his Twickenham kick-off that winning run was set to end. Stoop fed Ronnie Poulton whose cross kick was collected by Gloucester front rower Harry Berry. Scrum half Dai Gent fed Redruth centre Barney Soloman, who fed Westoe wing Fred Chapman who burst through to score at the north end. What a start for the new ground.

England went on to win 11–6 and pip Wales to the title.

— LEADING FROM THE FRONT —

Arthur Gould led Wales 18 times in 27 appearances to set the standard for future Welsh captains to follow. The Newport star played his last game on 9th January 1897 when he led his side to victory over England at Rodney Parade by 11–0.

Ieuan Evans finally surpassed his record 97 years later on 17th May 1994 at Lisbon University when he led Wales for the 19th time in a 102–11 victory over Portugal in a Rugby World Cup qualifying game. Evans went on to stretch his record to 28 games as captain. For the record, there had been 123 captains of Wales up to 18th August 2007.

Games as capt	Name	W	D	L
28	Ieuan Evans	13	0	15
22	Rob Howley	15	0	7
22	Colin Charvis	11	0	11
19	Jonathan Humphreys	6	0	13
18	Arthur Gould	8	1	9
18	Gareth Thomas	9	0	9
14	Clive Rowlands	6	2	6
14	Billy Trew	12	0	2

— FAMILY FEUD —

Aberavon's father and son forward pair, George and Walter Vickery, hold a rare distinction – they both played against Ireland, but for different countries. George won his one cap with England in a 17–3 defeat by the Irish in Cork on 11th February 1905.

Walter, who was a docker, made his debut for Wales against his father's country, England, on 15th January 1938. He played throughout the championship campaign and won his fourth and final cap against England at Twickenham the following season.

— IF AT FIRST YOU DON'T SUCCEED . . . —

The Championship game between Scotland and Wales in 1899 was postponed no fewer than four times because of bad weather. It was eventually played at Inverleith, Edinburgh, on 4th March. The Scots won 21–10 after Wales had led 10–3 at half-time following a first-half played in a snow storm.

— THE LAST MINER —

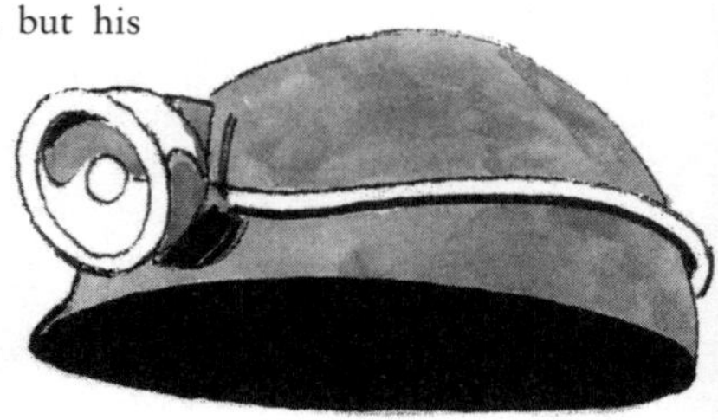

Garin Jenkins won 58 caps, but his proudest claim to fame is that he was the last miner to play for Wales. Having won his first cap against France in 1991, Jenkins finished as Wales' most capped hooker when he played his last game against South Africa in 2000.

The Swansea hooker was the 126th member of the mining and coal industry in Wales to play international rugby, a tradition that began with Cardiff forward Arthur Jones in 1883.

Miners to win ten or more caps for Wales are:

Jack Bassett	(15 caps, 1929–32 – Penarth)
Lonza Bowdler	(15 caps, 1927–33 – Cross Keys)
Bobby Brice	(18 caps, 1899–1904 – Aberavon/Cardiff)
Billy Cleaver	(14 caps, 1947–50 – Cardiff)
Cliff Davies	(16 caps, 1947–51 – Cardiff)
Dai Davies	(17 caps, 1950–54 – Somerset Police)
Jehoida Hodges	(23 caps 1899–1906 – Newport)
Garin Jenkins	(58 caps, 1991–2000 – Pontypool/Swansea)
Dai 'Tarw' Jones	(13 caps, 1902–06 – Treherbert)
Jack Jones	(14 caps, 1908–20 – Newport/Pontypool))
Staff Jones	(10 caps, 1983–88 – Pontypool)
Ivor Morgan	(13 caps, 1908–12 – Swansea)
Dai Morris	(34 caps, 1967–74 – Neath)
Steve Morris	(19 caps, 1920–25 – Cross Keys)
John Perkins	(18 caps, 1983–86 – Pontypool)
Russell Robins	(13 caps, 1953–57 – Pontypridd)
Glyn Shaw	(12 caps, 1972–77 – Neath)
Archie Skym	(20 caps, 1928–35 – Llanelli/Cardiff)
Glyn Stephens	(10 caps, 1912–13 – Neath)
Bill 'Bunner' Travers	(12 caps, 1937–49 – Newport)
George Travers	(25 caps, 1903–11 – Pill Harriers/Newport)
Jim Webb	(20 caps, 1907–12 – Abertillery)
Jeff Whitefoot	(19 caps, 1984–87 – Cardiff)

— MEN OF THE DECADES, 1880s: ARTHUR GOULD —

Arthur Gould came from a remarkable sporting family. His parents moved from Oxford during the industrial revolution and three of their sons played for Wales. A fourth captained Newport and ran in the Olympic Games for Great Britain and six Goulds played for Newport.

But it was Joseph Arthur Gould, known as Arthur or 'Monkey' – he got his nickname because of his amazing agility and love of climbing trees as a youngster – who was the brightest star of them all. In fact, the Newport centre can lay claim to being rugby's first 'superstar'.

Gould was rugby's equivalent of the cricketing idol, Dr W.G. Grace. He was featured in countless newspapers, pen portraits and even had his picture on the front of boxes of matches. Born in Newport on 10th October 1864, it didn't take long for him to make his mark. When Newport were one short for their trip to Weston-super-Mare the groundsman, John Butcher, invited the 16-year-old Arthur Gould to play at full back.

He was given strict instructions to kick the ball whenever he got it, but instead ran at every opportunity and ended up with two of his side's three tries. So began one of the greatest careers in Welsh rugby history and he was never dropped by his club.

He helped Newport win the South Wales Challenge Cup, dropped 20 goals in 1885/86, scored 31 tries in the Invincible season of 1891/92, won a world record 27 caps for Wales and captained his country a record 18 times.

He was Newport skipper for three seasons and led Wales to their first Triple Crown. From 1885 to1897 he was assured of his place in the Welsh team, even though he roamed around the country and played at various times for Southampton Trojans, London Welsh, Richmond, Hampshire, South Wales and Middlesex. He also missed the whole of 1891 international campaign because he was away on business in the West Indies.

Arthur was also a fine athlete and a useful cricketer. On the track, he won £1,000 in foot races alone and was Midland Counties' 100 yards and 120 yards hurdles champion in 1892.

Arthur's final season, 16 years on from his debut, was in 1896/97. He headed the Newport scorers again with seven tries and nine dropped goals in 13 appearances and had his final outing for Wales. That season saw a local newspaper set up a testimonial fund for Arthur and the WRU endorsed and supported the scheme. Such was the backing that the President of the WRU, Sir John Llewellyn, was able to present the Welsh skipper with the title deeds to his home at 6 Llanthewy Road, Newport.

The other unions were furious and the Scots and Irish refused to play Wales that season claiming Gould was now a professional. It meant the curtain fell on Arthur's illustrious career at Rodney Parade on 9th January, 1897, when he led Wales for one final time against England on his home ground of Rodney Parade. Wales won 11–0, the International Rugby Board entered the row and assurances were sought of the WRU that they would never pick Arthur again. The WRU stood firm, backing their man, but Arthur promptly retired to save everyone's blushes.

It wasn't the end of Arthur's involvement in rugby. No sooner had he retired than he became a member of the WRU Match Committee, helping to select Welsh teams, and he also refereed.

— WALES' RECORD IN THE 1880s —

Played 19 Won 5 Drew 2 Lost 12
Tries: 16–57
Win percentage: 26.32%
Beat New Zealand Natives 1888
Most appearances: Tom Clapp (Newport) 14
Most tries: Henry Jordan (Newport), Tom Clapp (Newport) 2
Most games as captain: Charles Newman (Newport) 6
Most individual wins: Tom Clapp (Newport), Buller Stadden (Dewsbury) 4

— HOME TRUTHS —

Wales played their first home game against England at St Helen's, Swansea on 16th December 1882. It was a game that was full of 'firsts'. Not only did international rugby make its bow on Welsh soil, but it was the first international match refereed by a Welshman, David Herbert. It turned out to be his one and only international.

The game, handsomely won by England by two goals and four tries to nil, also featured the Championship's first hat-trick of tries, by Oxford University three-quarter Gregory Wade.

The only other Wales game to be refereed by a Welshman was on 3rd January 1885, also against England at Swansea, when Charles Lewis took charge of an England victory by one goal and five tries to one goal and two tries.

— WELSH CAP NUMBERS —

From the first player capped for Wales to the 1,000th, here are some of the landmarks reached along the way:

Number 1: JAMES BEVAN, 1881 (v England at Blackheath)
Australian-born Bevan was the captain of Wales in their first international match. A Cambridge University student, who resided in Grosmont, near Abergavenny, he later became a clergyman. It was his one and only cap.

Number 100: STEPHEN THOMAS, 1890 (v Scotland at Cardiff)
Capped three times in the Wales pack whilst playing for Llanelli. He was a tinplate worker.

Number 200: SID BEVAN, 1904 (v Ireland at Belfast)
A metal broker from Swansea, he won only one cap. He played for the Lions in four Tests against Australia and New Zealand later that year. He served in the First World War as a lieutenant.

Number 300: BEN BEYNON, 1920 (v England at Swansea)
Played soccer for Swansea, scoring the goal that knocked Blackburn out of the FA Cup in 1915, and was outside half for the rugby club. He joined Oldham RL in 1925 and won a Challenge Cup Final winners medal.

Number 400: DAVID JENKINS, 1926 (v England at Cardiff)
A forward from Swansea, he played in all four matches of 1926 before joining Hunslet RLFC that summer. Played twice for the Wales rugby league side.

Number 500: BARNEY McCALL, 1936 (v England at Swansea)
Born in Clifton, he had no Welsh blood but won three caps while serving in the Welsh Regiment. He became the Cadet Force Executive Officer in Glamorgan and won a Military Cross in the Second World War. Played cricket for Dorset, Combined Services and the Army.

Number 600: LEN DAVIES, 1954 (v France at Cardiff)
The elder brother of full back Terry Davies, he played three times as a blindside wing forward, before his untimely death at the age of 26.

Number 700: JOHN LLOYD, 1966 (v England at Twickenham)
A superb ball-handling Bridgend prop who won 24 caps in eight years, and captained his country three times in 1972. He became Wales coach in 1979.

Number 800: MALCOLM DACEY, 1983 (v England at Cardiff)
Played at fly half, centre and full back for Wales while at Swansea. He featured in the 1987 Rugby World Cup and appeared for a British Lions team against the Rest of World in Cardiff in 1986.

Number 1,000: MICHAEL OWEN, 2002 (v South Africa at Bloemfontein)
The Pontypridd player became Wales' 1,000th cap when Steve Hansen gave him a debut at blindside flanker in South Africa. Now with the Dragons, he skippered Wales to the Grand Slam in 2005, after Gareth Thomas was injured, and toured with the Lions to New Zealand.

— CURLY HAIRED MARMOSETS —

Evan and David James were nicknamed 'the curly-haired marmosets' because of their flamboyant style on the field. They played at half-back together for Wales four times and were worshipped in Swansea, where they invented half-back play.

Labourers in the local copper works, they were known to take to the field at St Helen's doing somersaults. They rocked the nation in 1892 when they announced they were joining Broughton Rangers in the Northern Union.

The WRU declared the Jameses to be professionals – Broughton were renowned for paying generous expenses – although they relented four years later and reinstated the brothers as amateurs. That led to one final fling for Wales against England in 1899.

The two brothers led England a merry dance in a 26–3 win at St Helen's, even though Evan had a dislocated shoulder. The RFU complained bitterly and 12 days later the two re-signed for Broughton for £200 each, £2 per game and jobs as warehousemen.

Three more brothers from the same family, Sam, Willie and Claude, all joined Broughton and Sam and Willie won international honours under Northern Union auspices. In the 1902 Challenge Cup final against Salford, Sam and Willie were both on the winning side, Willie kicking four goals in a 25–0 victory.

— WOODY'S WEMBLEY WOES —

Wembley wizard Scott Gibbs

The match between Wales and England at Wembley on April 11th 1999 was one of the most remarkable in Five Nations history. With five minutes to go, and his team leading 31–25, it seemed pretty certain to Clive Woodward that his England side would be picking up their 12th Grand Slam, record fifth successive Triple Crown and the Five Nations title. Wales had battled back gamely in the second half, but it would take something extraordinary to rob England of their prize.

No wonder, then, that Woodward, unfamiliar with the surroundings at Wales' temporary home, turned to a steward and asked which way his players should go up to the Royal Box to receive the trophy. At that very moment the Five Nations trophy was being brought to the Royal Box by a Welsh Rugby Union official to allow it to be presented to Lawrence Dallaglio.

But no sooner had Woodward turned back to the game than something extraordinary happened. Neil Jenkins kicked a penalty down the line to the English 22 – it was the second minute of injury time. Wales won a four-man line-out through Chris Wyatt, Scott Quinnell went on a decoy run and Scott Gibbs took up the running.

Gibbs had already been a Challenge Cup winner at Wembley with St Helens, but now he was on course for something even more special – a wonder try to break the hearts of the English and hand the title to the Scots. Gibbs bobbed, weaved and sidestepped his way past five English defenders before scoring half-way out on the right. Wales were a point behind with the conversion to come.

As the Welsh players mobbed the try scorer, Gibbs walked up to Jenkins and slapped the ball in his hands: "Now kick it," he said. Jenkins didn't fail him, and ended up with 22 points in the game, as Wales turned the championship on its head with an incredible 32–31 triumph.

As soon as Jenkins added his conversion the WRU official had to quietly retrieve the trophy – with a hint of a smile on his face!

— WELSH SPORT'S MR FIX IT —

The first Secretary of the WFRU was Richard Mullock, a man who had his fingers in many sporting pies. As well as being a founder member of the Newport Athletic Club in 1874, he was also present at the formation of the Amateur Atheltics Association (AAA) at the Randolph Hotel, Oxford in 1880.

In 1881, he took it upon himself to select a Welsh rugby team to play against England. His side was hammered and a month later the Welsh Rugby Football Union was formed in Neath.

Mullock was elected Honorary Secretary and Treasurer and served as Secretary until 1892. He became Wales' fourth international referee when he 'umpired' the 1885 championship clash between Ireland and England at Lansdowne Road.

He was frequently found in the summer umpiring cricket matches at Newport and was elected to the AAA general committee in 1881 as a representative of the 'West of England' clubs.

— OUT OF THE BLACK INTO THE RED —

The early representative teams from Wales, selected by the South Wales Football Union, wore black shirts with a white leek slashed boldly across the front.

The first Welsh team that met England in 1881, selected by Richard Mullock, wore scarlet jerseys bearing the Prince of Wales feathers. This followed the adoption of the logo by the Welch Regiment in 1719 and the London Cymmrodorion Society in 1751.

Wales have played in scarlet jerseys ever since, although in modern times there have been change strips for away games and the logo was stylised and trademarked in December 1991. Here are the occasions on which Wales have not played in red shirts, the first being 29th May 1987 during the first Rugby World Cup when they turned out against Tonga in green shirts.

Green	
v Tonga (Palmerston North, 29th May 1987)	Won 29–16
v Canada (Invercargill, 3rd Jun 1987)	Won 40–9
v USA (Cardiff, 7th Nov 1987)	Won 46–0
v Japan (Cardiff, 16th Oct 1993)	Won 55–5
v Canada (Cardiff, 10th Nov 1993)	Lost 24–26
v Japan (Bloemfontein, 27th May 1995)	Won 57–10
v Canada (Cardiff, 21st Aug 1999)	Won 33–19
Ecru	
v US Eagles (Cardiff, 11th Jan 1997)	Won 34–14
v US Eagles (Wilmington, 5th Jul 1997)	Won 30–20
v US Eagles (San Francisco, 12th Jul 1997)	Won 28–23
v Canada (Toronto, 19th Jul 1997)	Won 28–25
v Tonga (Swansea, 16th Nov 1997)	Won 46–12
Black	
v Tonga (Cardiff, 17th Nov 2001)	Won 51–7
v Canada (Cardiff, 16th Nov 2002)	Won 32–21
v Fiji (Cardiff, 11th Nov 2005)	Won 11–10
v Australia (Cardiff, 26th Nov 2005)	Won 24–22
White	
v Canada (Melbourne, 12th Oct 2003)	Won 41–10
v Romania (Cardiff, 12th Nov 2004)	Won 66–7
v Japan (Cardiff, 26th Nov 2004)	Won 98–0
v Canada (Toronto, 11th Jun 2005)	Won 60–3
Grey	
v Canada (Cardiff, 17th Nov 2006)	Won 61–26

— MEN OF THE DECADES: THE 1890s, BILLY BANCROFT —

Billy Bancroft was one of the first professionals to play rugby union. It wasn't with the oval ball that he earned his living, however, but with the cricket bat and ball. Both his grandfather and father, William senior and junior, were fine cricketers with William senior being the Swansea CC professional. William junior also played for Glamorgan, Swansea and South Wales CC.

Billy scored 8,353 runs, including seven centuries, between1889 and 1914 as one of the leading professionals for Glamorgan during their Minor Counties era. A useful change bowler, he took a hat-trick and scored a century against Surrey 2nd X1 at Swansea in 1899 and helped Glamorgan become joint Minor Counties champions in 1900.

In 1895, when he was 24, he was appointed the professional with Glamorgan on the princely sum of £2 per week for 20 weeks. The man who appointed him was Sir John Llewellyn, the President of both the Swansea rugby club and the Welsh Rugby Union.

He scored a match-winning 71 in Glamorgan's first Minor Counties victory over Cornwall in Swansea in 1897, scored a half-century against the touring South Africans in 1901, played for Glamorgan against Australia in 1902, hit 207 against Berkshire in 1903 and played for the South Wales X1 against Australia again in 1909.

Brought up in the cottage adjoining St Helen's, he lived most of his life in and around the famous home of Swansea cricket and rugby club. At the end of his playing career he became groundsman and, in the inter-war period, acted as a steward in the members' enclosure.

On the rugby front, he played at full back for Wales in 33 successive internationals between1890 and 1901 – a world record – making his debut at 19 in his first season of senior rugby. He claimed another world record on 4th March 1899 when he surpassed English legend Lennard Stokes' Test points mark of 40 with two conversions in a defeat by the Scots in Edinburgh. He eventually took his Welsh points tally to 60, a then world record.

He was in the first Welsh team to win the Championship and Triple Crown in 1890 and he also landed the Championship's first penalty, with a drop kick in the win over England at the Arms Park. Bancroft was captain of the side that won Wales' second Triple Crown in 1900, making him the first Welshman to capture two Crowns, and he captained his country in his last 11 Tests (seven wins and four defeats) to set another Welsh record that was finally broken by Clive Rowlands in 1965.

Bancroft joined Swansea rugby club in 1889 and went on to captain them for no fewer than six seasons. He scored more than 1,000 points for the club. Despite all his successes on the cricket and rugby fields, Billy often claimed his proudest sporting achievement came when his protégé, Gilbert Parkhouse, played cricket for England.

He died the day after his 88th birthday on 3rd March 1959.

— WALES' RECORD IN THE 1890s —

Played 27 Won 11 Drew 1 Lost 15
Tries: 34–55
Win percentage: 40.74%
Triple Crown in 1893
Outright Championship win in 1893
Most appearances: Billy Bancroft (Swansea) 27
Most tries: Willie Llewellyn (Llwynypia) 5
Most points: Billy Bancroft (Swansea) 43
Most games as captain: Arthur Gould (Newport) 17

— TRIPLE CROWN DISASTER —

The celebrations after John Gwilliam's side had won the first Triple Crown in 39 years with their 6–3 victory over Ireland in Belfast on 11th March 1950 should have gone on for many days. But they were cruelly cut short the next day when a Tudor V aircraft carrying Welsh rugby fans back home crashed at Llandow, near Cardiff, and killed 80 people. At the time, it was the worst disaster in aviation history.

There were three survivors, one of whom was 33-year-old Handel Rogers, from Llanelli. He went on to become President of the Welsh Rugby Union in 1976 and went back to Dublin to see Wales secure another Triple Crown that year.

Two weeks after the accident five uniformed buglers played the 'Last Post' before Wales completed the Grand Slam with a 21–0 win over France at the Arms Park. An appeal fund raised £40,000.

— TOP TRY THOMAS —

Gareth Thomas stretched his Wales try record to 38 on the same day he overtook Gareth Llewellyn's Welsh cap record when he scored in the first Test against Australia in Sydney on 26th May 2007.

Thomas scored four tries in a Test match against Italy and ran in five against Western Australia in a tour game in Perth on 29th May 1996. As well as his 39 Test tries, Thomas also had eight tries to add from ten further appearances in a Welsh jersey.

10 tries or more for Wales:

No	Name	Career	Caps	Tries
1	Gareth Thomas	1995–2007	91+5	39
2	Ieuan Evans	1987–1998	72	33
3	Shane Williams	2000–2007	43+3	29
4=	Gerald Davies	1966–1978	46	20
4=	Gareth Edwards	1967–1978	53	20
4=	Colin Charvis	1996–2007	80+8	20
7	Rhys Williams	2000–2005	35+9	18
8=	Reggie Gibbs	1906–1911	16	17
8=	Johnny Williams	1906–1911	17	17
8=	Tom Shanklin	2001–2007	33+9	17
8=	Ken Jones	1947–1957	44	17
12	Willie Llewellyn	1899–1905	20	16
13=	Teddy Morgan	1902–1908	16	14
13=	Dafydd James	1996–2006	39+8	14
15=	Nigel Walker	1993–1998	16+1	12
15=	Arwel Thomas	1996–2000	19+4	12
15=	JJ Williams	1973–1979	29+1	12
18=	Rhys Gabe	1901–1908	24	11
18=	Billy Trew	1900–1913	29	11
18=	Dewi Bebb	1959–1967	34	11
18=	Wayne Proctor	1992–2001	37+2	11
18=	Kevin Morgan	1997–2007	41+3	11
18=	Scott Quinnell	1993–2002	50+2	11
18=	Mark Taylor	1994–2005	49+3	11
18=	Neil Jenkins	1991–2002	81+6	11
26=	Mark Jones	2001–2007	29+1	10
26=	Allan Bateman	1990–2001	31+4	10
26=	Scott Gibbs	1991–2001	53	10
26=	Rob Howley	1996–2002	58+1	10
26=	Martyn Williams	1996–2007	61+10	10

— A FULL HOUSE —

Where Jerry Shea led against England in Swansea in 1920, only two other Welsh players have followed in completing a full house of modern scoring – try, conversion, penalty goal, drop goal – in a single match.

Neil Jenkins followed suit 81 years later in the win over France in Paris in 2001 and James Hook became the first Welshman to achieve the feat in Cardiff against England in 2007.

Four players have completed the full house against Wales. Wales lost on each of those occasions, but won thanks to the efforts of Shea, Jenkins and Hook.

Full house for Wales:

Name	Date	Opponent (Venue)	By*	Result
Jerry Shea	17th Jan 1920	England (Swansea)	43'	Won 19–5
Neil Jenkins	17th Mar 2001	France (Paris)	80'	Won 43–35
James Hook	17th Mar 2007	England (Cardiff)	68'	Won 27–18

Full house against Wales:

Name	Date	Opponent (Venue)	By*	Result
Guy Camberabero	1st Apr 1967	France (Paris)	78	Lost 14–20
Craig Chalmers	2nd Feb 1991	Scotland (Murrayfield)	53'	Lost 12–32
Felipe Contepomi	10th Nov 2001	Argentina (Cardiff)	69'	Lost 16–30
Jonny Wilkinson	23rd Mar 2002	England (Twickenham)	43'	Lost 10–50

* By = minute of match in which the feat was accomplished.

— CATCH OF THE DAY —

Gareth Edwards may have hung up his boots in 1978, but he remained a highly competitive sportsman. First there was TV's *Superstars* and then fishing. In 1990 he set a British angling record when he landed a 45lbs 6oz pike at Llandegfedd reservoir.

— POISONED ARROW FELLS YOUNGEST CAP —

Norman Biggs became the youngest player ever to don the Welsh jersey when he made his debut against the New Zealand Natives at the age of 18 years and 50 days on 22nd December 1888.

It proved to be a winning start to an eight-cap career that reached a crescendo in 1893 when he scored two tries in Wales' first Triple Crown season, by which time he was 22.

The son of a brewer who had businesses in Cardiff and Bath, Biggs captained both clubs and was one of six brothers who played for Cardiff. In fact, a Biggs played for the Cardiff 1st XV for 22 consecutive seasons.

Norman also played cricket for Glamorgan alongside his brother Selwyn, who won nine Welsh caps. A police officer in the Glamorgan Constabulary, he served as a private in the Glamorgan Yeomanry in the Boer War and was a superintendent in the Nigerian police force when he was killed by a poisoned arrow during a native ambush in Sakaba, Nigeria in February 1908. He was 37.

Wales' 18-year-old caps:

Norman Biggs	v New Zealand Natives, 1888	18 yrs 49 days
Evan Williams	v England, 1925	18 yrs 213 days
Harry Bowen	v England 1882	18 yrs 226 days
Tom Pearson	v England 1891	18 yrs 238 days
Lewis Jones	v England, 1950	18 yrs 285 days
Will H. Thomas	v Scotland, 1885	18 yrs 294 days
Keith Jarrett	v England, 1967	18 yrs 332 days
Edward Treharne	v England, 1881	18 yrs 334 days
Billy Bancroft	v Scotland, 1890	18 yrs 336 days
Haydn Tanner	v New Zealand, 1935	18 yrs 346 days
Frank Hill	v Scotland, 1885	18 yrs 363 days

The exact birth dates for the following players have never been established, but they were 18 when they made their debuts:

Bob Gould	v Ireland, 1882
Llewellyn Lloyd	v Ireland, 1896

— SOCK IT TO THEM —

When Wales played France at the Arms Park in 1994, team manager Rob Norster insisted on breaking with tradition and sending his side into battle with green rather than red socks.

Why? Because Norster had noticed in a previous game with Les Bleus that the referee had become confused at rucks and mauls with both teams wearing red socks. "It had cost us a couple of penalties in Paris the previous year and we wanted to ensure a greater distinction between the two teams," said Norster.

It was just as well Norster made the change or one of the greatest tries scored by a Welsh forward might have been overruled. Wales hadn't beaten France for 12 years, but came into the game with victories over Scotland and Ireland behind them.

The 21-year-old Scott Quinnell scored the first of Wales' two tries in the first-half when he broke from a line-out and raced up the right hand touchline. He fended off three tacklers before diving in at the corner as the cover defence closed him down. There was no doubt he touched down the ball for the try, but Irish touch judge Dave McHugh had to decide whether the mass of legs that had crossed the touchline belonged to Quinnell or the French defenders.

After initially putting up his flag he quickly took it down again when he realised the legs that had crossed the line were wearing red socks.

The try stood, Wales won 24–15 and went on to win the official Five Nations trophy for the first time.

— OLD HEADS MAKE IT A TRIPLE TRIPLE CROWN —

John Dawes sent in the old guard to ensure Wales became the first country to make it three Triple Crowns in a row. The Wales coach selected the oldest Welsh team ever to take to the field for the assignment at Lansdowne Road, Dublin on 4th March 1978.

Pontypool prop Charlie Faulkner, one of four '30-somethings', was the oldest player at 37 and the average age for the 15 starters was 29 years, 213 days. They beat Ireland 20–16 and went on to secure the Grand Slam against France in Cardiff two weeks later.

— ARMS PARK HEROES —

Ievan Evans: More Arms Park tries than any other player

- J.P.R. Williams holds the record for the most international victories for Wales at Cardiff Arms Park (1884–1997). The London Welsh and Bridgend full back tasted success in 24 of the 29 matches he played at the home of Welsh rugby.
- But Ieuan Evans played more games at the Arms Park, or National Ground as it became known during his era, during his 72-cap career. The Llanelli wing played 32 times at the ground, winning 13 times and drawing once.

- Evans holds the record for the most Test tries at the Arms Park – 16, at an average of one every two games – while Neil Jenkins amassed 242 points at an average of 11 per each of his 22 games.
- Swansea scrum half Dickie Owen and Newport hooker George Travers won on all nine appearances at the Arms Park, while Terry Cobner enjoyed eight wins and a draw.
- Since the Millennium Stadium opened in 1999, Gareth Thomas and Colin Charvis lead the way tied on 37 appearances, but Thomas is ahead with 20 wins.
- Stephen Jones is the leading points scorer with 352 from 35 matches, while Shane Williams has harvested 13 tries in 26 matches to equal Evans' Arms Park strike rate.

— TOM THE IMPRESARIO —

Llywnypia solicitor Tom Williams holds a special place in Welsh rugby history for instigating the singing of the Welsh national anthem, as a response to the Haka, ahead of the game against New Zealand in 1905.

Williams played for Pontypridd, Cardiff and Llwynypia and was capped once for Wales in the first international victory against Ireland in Dublin in 1882. He became a member of the WRU in 1899, serving the Mid District, and refereed the 1904 international between England and Ireland. A member of the IRB between1901 and 1908, he became a vice-president of the WRU in 1910. He was a national selector, although probably abstained when it came to discussing the merits of his nephew, Willie Llewellyn.

It was Williams who hatched the plan to try to get the crowd to join the Welsh players in singing 'Hen Wlad fy Nhadau' after the Maori war cry had been delivered. He wrote to the Western Mail and expressed the wish that the fans would join in the response to the New Zealand challenge. The Welsh Regiment's 2nd Battalion Band played before the teams entered the packed arena and struck up 'Men of Harlech' as the All Blacks took to the field.

The Haka was first up before the Welsh players gathered in the centre of the field and began to sing the national anthem. It didn't take long for the crowd to join in and the most famous revered tradition of any international game at Cardiff Arms Park was launched.

— CARDIFF ARMS PARK STATS (1884–1997) —

Barry John: scored more Arms Park drop goals than any other player

Most games		W	D	L
32	Ieuan Evans	13	1	18
29	J.P.R. Williams	24	2	3
28	Gareth Edwards	23	2	3
26	Gareth Llewellyn	10	0	16
26	Robert Jones	9	0	17
22	Graham Price	18	1	3
21+1	Neil Jenkins	9	1	12
22	Gerald Davies	18	1	3
22	Phil Davies	10	1	11

By an opponent: 7, Willie John McBride (2-0-5), Mike Gibson (1-0-6), Philippe Sella (6–0-1), Rob Andrew (6 starts and a rep, 3-0-4)
Never lost: 9 wins, George Travers, Dickie Owen
Never won: 6 losses, Fergus Slattery

Most points

242	Neil Jenkins
171	Paul Thorburn
102	Phil Bennett

By an opponent: 31, Michael Kiernan; 30, Diego Dominguez; 28, Gavin Hastings, Rob Andrew

Most tries

16	Ieuan Evans
13	Gerald Davies
12	Gareth Edwards
9	J.J. Williams

By an opponent: 4, Philippe Sella; 3, Joost van der Westhuizen, Jim Renwick, Brendan Mullin, Jean-Baptiste Lafond, Serge Blanco, Howard Marshall

Most drop goals

6	Barry John
4	Gareth Davies
4	Jonathan Davies
3	Steve Fenwick

By an opponent: 2, Michel Vannier, Nim Hall, Rob Andrew

— THE LONG RUN-IN —

It used to be the prize of Newport wing Stuart Watkins, with his 75-yard interception try against France at Cardiff Arms Park in 1966, but Gareth Thomas added 20 yards to his record against Australia 30 years later to claim the longest interception try in Welsh international history.

Thomas was playing at centre when he intercepted a George Gregan pass in the shadow of his own posts and sped virtually the length of the field for a try.

It inspired a Welsh fightback from 18–9 down. Momentarily, Wales led 19–18 midway through the second half, but the Wallabies hit back to win 28–19. Nothing less would have done for them on the day that one of the game's all-time greats played his final Test. It was goodbye to David Campese after 64 tries and 101 caps.

— MILLENNIUM STADIUM STATS (1999–APRIL 2007) —

Most games		W	D	L
35+2	Gareth Thomas	20	1	16
34+3	Colin Charvis	19	1	17
32+3	Stephen Jones	16	2	17
29+5	Martyn Williams	17	2	15
23+3	Shane Williams	14	2	10
17+8	Dwayne Peel	15	2	8
16+6	Rhys Williams	11	0	11
21+2	Ian Gough	11	2	10

By an opponent: 5, Scott Murray (1-0-4); 4+1 Chris Paterson (1-0-4), Fabien Pelous (4-0-1), Pieter de Villiers (4-0-1)

Most points

352	Stephen Jones
180	Neil Jenkins
65	Shane Williams

By an opponent: 53, Dan Carter; 37, Percy Montgomery; 35, David Humphreys; 30, Jonny Wilkinson, Matt Burke

Most Tries

13	Shane Williams
12	Rhys Williams
11	Gareth Thomas
10	Tom Shanklin
7	Dafydd James

By an opponent: 4, Will Greenwood; 3, Sitaveni Sivivatu, Rico Gear

Most drop goals

No Welshman has more than one.
By an opponent: 2, Jonny Wilkinson

— HAPPY BIRTHDAY —

- Gwyn Rowlands certainly had a day to remember on 19th December 1953. Not only did he notch his second win over the touring All Blacks, but he won his first cap on his 25th birthday. The Cardiff wing kicked a penalty and two conversions in the famous 13–8 win – he had scored a try and conversion in Cardiff's win a month earlier – to crown a great day. It remains the last time Wales beat New Zealand.
- Newport forward Jack Whitfield reached 30 on the same day Wales clinched the Championship title in Paris on 23rd March 1922. He crossed for his fourth try of the season to help Wales win 11–3.
- The only other birthday try scorer was Ospreys back row man Ryan Jones, who scored at Murrayfield during the 2005 Grand Slam campaign.
- Ieuan Evans is the only player to play for Wales on two birthdays. Both games were against Scotland and he lost at Murrayfield when he was 23 and won at the Arms Park when he was 28.
- Evans was captain in the latter match, as was Cliff Jones on his 24th birthday against Ireland in Swansea – his 13th and final cap before retiring.

Here's the full list of Wales' birthday boys:

Date	Name	Age	Opponents	Venue	Notes
14th Mar 1914	David Watts	28	Ireland	Belfast	
21st Jan 1922	Brinley Evans	28	England	Cardiff	
23rd Mar 1922	Jack Whitfield	30	France	Paris	Try
2nd Feb 1924	Gwyn Francis	28	Scotland	Inverleith	
27th Mar 1924	Edward Watkins	25	France	Paris	
16th Jan 1926	Ron Herrera	21	England	Cardiff	
16th Jan 1932	Watcyn Thomas	26	England	Swansea	
12th Mar 1938	Cliff Jones	24	Ireland	Swansea	Capt
7th Apr 1951	Cliff Morgan	21	France	Paris	
19th Dec 1953	Gwyn Rowlands*	25	New Zealand	Cardiff	2c,1p
16th Jan 1960	John Collins	29	England	Twickenham	
26th Mar 1960	Norman Morgan	25	France	Cardiff	1c,1p
7th Feb 1976	Gerald Davies	31	Scotland	Cardiff	
2nd Mar 1985	Rob Ackerman	24	Scotland	Murrayfield	
1st Mar 1986	Adrian Hadley	23	France	Cardiff	

14th Jun 1986	Stuart Evans	23	Samoa	Apia	
21st Mar 1987	Ieuan Evans	23	Scotland	Murrayfield	
18th Mar 1989	Mike Griffiths	27	England	Cardiff	
21st Mar 1992	Ieuan Evans	28	Scotland	Cardiff	Capt
5th Jun1993	Lyn Jones	29	Namibia	Windhoek	
18th Mar 1995	Mike Griffiths	33	Ireland	Cardiff	
13th Oct 2001	Rob Howley	31	Ireland	Cardiff	
21st Jun 2003	Robert Sidoli	24	New Zealand	Hamilton	
26th Feb 2005	Shane Williams	28	France	Paris	
13th Mar 2005	Ryan Jones	24	Scotland	Murrayfield	Try
17th Nov 2006	Gethin Jenkins	26	Canada	Cardiff	

* Debut

— WHAT'S MISSING? —

A manufacturer's error before Wales' Five Nations match with England at Twickenham on 18th January 1958 meant that the away team were supplied with red trial jerseys instead of the fully fledged, and badged, international shirts.

"I don't think anyone realised before, during or after the match. It was amazing," said WRU Secretary, Bill Clement.

Wales drew 3–3 thanks to a 45-yard penalty from Llanelli full back Terry Davies.

— WHO SCORED? —

Ireland visited St Helen's, Swansea on 8th March 1930 to take on Wales in the Five Nations Championship. Ireland were leading 4–3 in the first half when Welsh forward Harry Peacock, of Newport, and Swansea wing Howie Jones dived simultaneously to record the only joint try awarded in international history.

It was Jones's debut and the only time he would get over the whitewash in a two-match career, whilst the only other try Peacock had scored was on his own debut against Scotland also at St Helen's the year before.

— MEN OF THE DECADES, THE 1900s: ERITH GWYNNE NICHOLLS —

The gates at the entrance to Cardiff Arms Park bear testimony to the way the people of Cardiff and Wales felt about their most famous adopted son. The Gwyn Nicholls Memorial Gates celebrate the life, times and great achievements of the man who was christened the 'Prince of Wales' centres.

Born in Westbury on Severn, Erith Gwynne Nicholls almost had an unfortunate start to his life when the first name put down on his birth certificate was 'Edith'. It was quickly erased and substituted with 'Erith', although he was known throughout his playing career as 'Gwyn'.

The statistics of his 16-season career reveal his true greatness. There were 111 tries in 242 games for Cardiff – the family moved to Wales when Gwyn was five – 11 unbeaten appearances for Newport, 24 Tests and three tries for Wales and four Tests and two tries for the British Lions in a series triumph in Australia.

He captained Wales ten times, including most famously the 1905 victory over New Zealand. He captained the Triple Crown-winning side in 1902 and played a part in the Crowns of 1900 and 1905 as Welsh rugby entered its first 'Golden Era'.

With Willie Llewellyn, Rhys Gabe and Teddy Morgan he formed arguably the greatest Welsh three-quarter line of all time. They played together seven times, never lost and scored 16 tries.

But it was for his part in the win over New Zealand – the first Test match defeat suffered by the All Blacks in their history – that led to him joining Arthur Gould as one off the gods of the Welsh game. Wales went into the game, in December 1905, as the reigning Triple Crown champions and had the honour of northern hemisphere rugby riding on their performance after Dave Gallaher's side had swept all before them. Nicholls was captain of a team that contained his business partner, Bert Winfield, at full back. They strolled into their Victoria Laundry offices on the morning of the match to kill time and steady their nerves and were pleased to see a black cat wander in. They both stroked it and rode their luck later that afternoon.

Nicholls then delivered a stirring team talk before Wales took the field: "Gather round men. The eyes of the rugby world are on Wales today. It is up to us to prove that the Old Country is not quite barren of a team that is capable of giving New Zealand at least a hard fight. Every man in possession must be put down, ball and all. As for the forwards, you already know what to do to get the loose head. Come on! Let's get out."

The 3–0 victory made Nicholls and his team immortals of Welsh rugby. He scored a try for Cardiff in their 10–8 defeat by Gallaher's men a few weeks later and another in the sensational 17–0 win over the Springboks in 1907.

Captain of Cardiff for four seasons, he was a member of the club committee for 14 years and also served on the WRU General Committee. A Welsh selector for six seasons, he also refereed one international match in 1909 between England and Scotland at Twickenham. "Wasn't I awful," he declared after Scotland had won 18–8. He never refereed another Test again. His playing career, by contrast, was truly great.

— WALES' RECORD IN THE 1900s —

Played 35 Won 28 Drew 1 Lost 6
Tries: 116–43
Win Percentage: 80%
Grand Slams/Triple Crowns in 1908, 1909 and triple Crowns in 1900, 1902, 1905
Outright Championship wins in 1900, 1902, 1905, 1908, 1909
Beat New Zealand 1905 (3–0), Australia 1908 (9–6)
Most appearances: Dickie Owen (Swansea) 27
Most tries: Teddy Morgan (London Welsh) 12
Most points: Teddy Morgan (London Welsh) 36
Most games as captain: Gwyn Nicholls (Cardiff) 10
Most individual wins: Dickie Owen (Swansea) 21

— WHITE SHORTS —

Wales wore white shorts for the first time in their history against England at Cardiff Arms Park on 15th January 1949, having previously always worn black. When WRU Secretary Eric Evans produced them at the team run the day before the match they failed to meet with the approval of the captain, Haydn Tanner.

He wasn't worried about the colour, but was furious that the legs went virtually down to the knees. The midnight oil was burned by the seamstresses and the legs were shortened before kick-off the next day.

After that game, white shorts became the norm, other than for games in which the BBC asked Wales to revert to black shorts to help distinguish teams for those watching on black and white television sets.

— BRING ON THE ENGLISH! —

J.P.R.: Always a winner against England

Tough as teak full back J.P.R. Williams played against England 11 times between 1969–81 – and walked off a winner on every occasion. He missed the 1974 Five Nations match between the auld enemies through injury – and Wales lost 16–12 at Twickenham.

As a team, Wales made it a record nine successive home wins over England when J.P.R. won his then national record 54th cap in the 21–19 victory at the Arms Park in 1981.

J.P.R. also won on another occasion he played in England – serving, volleying, lobbing and smashing his way to the 1966 Junior Wimbledon tennis title.

— 100 AND OUT —

Neil Jenkins pulled on a Welsh jersey for the 100th and final time when he came on as a 64th minute replacement for Wales in the uncapped match against the Barbarians at the Millennium Stadium on 31st May 2003. His century of Welsh appearances was made up of 87 Tests, ten tour matches and three matches for a Wales XV.

Gareth Llewellyn ended with 106 Welsh appearances – 92 caps, ten tour matches and four matches for a Wales XV.

Record Welsh cap holder Gareth Thomas is another who has notched a century of Welsh appearances. He was still going strong in 2007 with 94 caps, eight tour games and two appearances for a Wales XV.

But nobody comes close to Jenkins in the points scoring stakes. He was the first player in world rugby to break through the 1,000 Test points barrier and scored 1,049 for Wales in his 87 internationals – more than three times the previous record of 304 held by Paul Thorburn.

100 points or more for Wales:

Name	Career	Caps	Tries	Conv	PG	DG	Mk	Pts
Neil Jenkins	1991–2002	81+6	11	130	235	10	-	1,049
Stephen Jones	1998–2007	55+7	6	95	103	3	-	538
Paul Thorburn	1985–1991	36+1	2	43	70	-	-	304
Arwel Thomas	1996–2000	19+4	12	30	32	-	-	216
Gareth Thomas	1995–2007	91+5	39	-	-	-	-	195
Phil Bennett	1969–1978	26+3	4	18	36	2	-	166
Ieuan Evans	1987–1998	72	33	-	-	-	-	157
Steve Fenwick	1975–1981	30	4	11	35	3	-	152
Shane Williams	2000–2007	43+3	29	-	-	-	-	145
Gavin Henson	2001–2007	15+7	3	29	18	1	-	130
Iestyn Harris	2001–2004	17+8	1	20	21	-	-	108
James Hook	2006–2007	12+2	3	20	14	2	-	103
Colin Charvis	1996–2007	80+8	20	-	-	-	-	100

— THE PERFECT 14 —

Gavin Henson put the boot into Japan at the Millennium Stadium in 2004 with a perfect 14 conversions of Wales' 14 tries in their 98–0 victory.

Neil Jenkins kicked a then world record 11 conversions in the 102–11 Rugby Wold Cup qualifying victory over Portugal in Lisbon in 1994, but he missed with five others.

— THE NORTHERN TWENTIES —

The economic depression in the twenties bit hard into everyday life in south Wales and had a devastating impact on Welsh rugby at the highest level. The coal industry halved the number of its workers from the 250,000 that had served it in 1920 and half a million people drifted out of Wales to find work elsewhere.

As a result, the twenties became the decade in which more players than any other drifted 'north' to play rugby league.

Wales topped the championship table in 1920, jointly with England and Scotland, but of the 21 players used in gaining three wins, five turned professional – Wick Powell, Jerry Shea, Brin Williams and George Oliver went to rugby league and Ben Beynon joined Swansea City to play football before turning to rugby league. Tom Parker's unbeaten Five Nations Championship-winning side of 1922 lost Fred Samuel and Will Bowen to the northern raiders. All in all, 37 Welsh internationals turned professional in the twenties.

The promise of a signing-on fee, win bonuses and a job was too much for many players to turn down. By the 1922/23 season there were up to 50 Welshmen appearing in the Northern Union. Pontypool began the 1921/22 season with only seven players having lost the majority of their pack to rugby league clubs, capped players Wilf Hodder and Oliver among them.

Decade	Number who turned pro
1890s	12
1900s	9
1910s	18
1920s	37
1930s	27
1940s	6
1950s	7
1960s	14
1970s	6
1980s	11
1990s	7
Total	**154**

— FIRST AND LAST WORD IN SCORING —

The scoring systems for rugby have changed down the years. Here is a list of the first and last scorers for the various points values for tries and goal kicks:

Tries

1pt try (**1890–1891**)
First: Arthur Gould (v Scotland, 1890)
Last: David Samuel (v Ireland, 1891)

2pt try (**1891–1893**)
First: Jim Hannan (v Scotland, 1892)
Last: Bert Gould (v Ireland, 1893)

3pt try (**1893–1971**)
First: Fred Parfitt (v England, 1894)
Last: Barry John (v France 1971)

4pt try (**1971–1992**)
First: J.P.R. Williams (v England, 1972)
Last: Richard Webster (v Scotland, 1992)

5pt try (**1992-now**)
First: Ieuan Evans (v England, 1993) *

* Wales played Italy on 7th October 1992 in an uncapped match at the Millennium Stadium. Anthony Clement scored the first of seven five-point tries.

Drop goals

3pt drop goal (**1890–91**)
First: Billy Bancroft (v Ireland, 1891)
Last: Billy Bancroft (v Ireland, 1891)

4pt drop goal (**1891–1948**)
First: Dai Fitzgerald (v Scotland, 1894)
Last: WTH Davies (v Ireland, 1939)

3pt drop goal (**1948–**)
First: Billy Cleaver (v Scotland, 1950)

Goals from mark

4pt goal from mark (**1891–1905**)
First: Billy Bancroft (v Scotland, 1895)
Last : Bert Winfield (v England, 1904)

3pt goal from mark (1905–1977)
First: Wick Powell (v England, 1931)
Last: Wick Powell (v England, 1931)

— ONE CAP WONDERS —

The 'One Cap Wonder' tag came into being right at the start of Welsh international history as no fewer than ten of the original team that faced England in 1881 never played again. A Wales rugby cap has always been the most coveted sporting trophy in the Principality and here are a few players who were delighted to get one:

- **Dr John Griffin** played his only game for Wales against Scotland on 8th January, 1886. Captain of Edinburgh University 3rd XV, he had no Welsh connection and had been born in Southampton. But the Welsh side arrived in Edinburgh one man short and Griffin was drafted in.
- **Nathan Rocyn Jones**, the St Mary's Hospital full back, played his only game for Wales in Belfast in 1925 when Ireland won 19–3. A Cambridge Blue in 1923, he went on to become the Honorary Medical Officer to the WRU and followed in the footsteps of his father, Sir David Rocyn Jones, in becoming the WRU President in 1964 .
- **Rex 'Tarzan' Richards** won his only cap against France at Cardiff Arms Park on 24th March 1956. The Cross Keys prop went on to become an exhibition high diver and Hollywood film actor, appearing in the film *The Wild Women of Wonga*.
- **Ray 'Chico' Hopkins** won one cap for Wales and one for the British Lions both as a replacement for the injured Gareth Edwards. The Maesteg scrum half's Welsh cap came at Twickenham on 28th February 1970. He made a try for JPR Williams and scored one himself to help Wales win 17–13.
- **Clive Shell** had the misfortune of being Gareth Edwards' understudy when Hopkins joined rugby league side Swinton. The Aberavon scrum half won his only cap when he replaced Edwards in injury time against Australia at the Arms Park in 1973.
- **William Elsey**, in 1895, and **Dan Jones**, in 1897, both marked their debuts with tries against England but were never selected again. Elsey, of Cardiff, ended up on the losing side, but Jones, who was the first cap from the Aberavon club, was a winner.

- **Willie Watts** captained Llanelli in 1913–14 and earned his first cap against England at Twickenham. He scored Wales' only try in a 10–9 defeat. Watts was wounded while serving in the First World War. He went on to become President of London Welsh RFC.
- **Bill Radford** still holds the record for being the oldest Welsh debutant at 35 years, 29 days. A back row forward who played in the Pill Harriers 'Invincible' side of 1918–19 and the unbeaten Newport team of 1922/23, he got his chance to play for Wales as one of five new caps in the final game of the 1923 championship campaign. It was against Ireland in Dublin and a number of players refused to travel because of the Irish Troubles. Wales lost 5–4 and before Wales played their next international Radford had died. He drowned in an accident at work at Newport docks.

— CAPTAINS ON DEBUT —

Only five players have skippered Wales on their international debut:

Year	Player	Opposition	Result
1881	James Bevan (Camb Uni)	England	Lost
1882	Charles Lewis (Llandovery)	Ireland	Won
1934	John Evans (Newport)	England	Lost
1963	Clive Rowlands (Pontypool)	England	Lost
1984	Mike Watkins (Newport)	Ireland	Won

— POLITICAL HELP —

The famous Welsh politician David Lloyd George was one of two MPs who kicked-off matches at Cardiff Arms Park in the 1907/08 season. He started the game between Cardiff and Blackheath on 25th January 1908, while the Irish MP John Redmond launched the fund-raising match between Billy Neill's Cardiff XV and a Rest of Wales XV on St Patrick's Day.

Lloyd George was the President of the Board of Trade at the time and on his way to becoming Prime Minister. His kick-off went the full 10 yards and was caught by Rhys Gabe – who promptly called for a mark. Cardiff beat Blackheath 19–3.

— RECORD RUN —

Wales' greatest run of victories came between 9th March 1907 and 1st January 1910. In that time they won 11 matches in a row and secured two 'unofficial' Grand Slams.

The run started with Wales' biggest winning margin against Ireland, 29–0, in Cardiff in a game which Welsh skipper Billy Trew withdrew from in protest at a suspension handed out to his Swansea team-mate Fred Scrine.

It was the only game in the 11-match run that Trew missed. The only other player to figure in ten games was Abertillery forward Jim Webb. He won his first cap in the defeat in Scotland prior to the Irish victory and promptly lost his place. Thereafter, he played 19 games in a row, playing with Trew through three Grand Slam seasons.

Over the 11 matches Wales scored 55 tries and conceded only 11. They scored 30 tries in three games against the French and were matched on try count on only one occasion – against the first touring Australian side in 1908 when each team scored two tries.

Wales won eight games in a row between 4th April 1970 and 25th March 1973, picking up the Grand Slam in 1971.That run included 22 tries with only seven against.

Rob Howley's team of 1999 came closest to matching the efforts of Trew and co with a ten-match winning streak between 6th March and 9th October. In fact, they also won an uncapped international during that period against the USA which made it 11 straight victories.

There were four away wins in the ten games – France, Italy and two Tests in Argentina – to match the four in the record 11-match winning streak. There were 32 tries scored and 19 against.

— ON YER BIKE, MIKE —

Wales and Lions prop forward Mike Griffiths missed the whole of the 1993 Five Nations Championship – after falling off a bicycle.

Griffiths was in Lanzarote with the Welsh squad for a spot of warm weather training in early January when he went for a mountain bike ride over the lunar-like lava surface of the island. Unfortunately, he was sent cartwheeling over the handlebars and broke his collarbone. Not only did he miss the entire championship, but it also put him out of the running for a second Lions tour and the trip to New Zealand that summer.

— FROM PITCH TO PULPIT —

Welsh internationals who later became ministers of the cloth:

James Bevan (1881)	Vicar of St George's, Great Yarmouth
Edward Peake (1881)	Rector at Bluntisham cum Erith
Alf Matthews (1886)	Vicar of Holy Trinity, Swansea
John Samuel (1891)	Life Deacon at Manselton Congregational Church
Albert Jenkin (1895–96)	Archdeacon of Pretoria
David Davies (1904)	Vicar of Eyeworth, Bedfordshire
Alban Davies (1913–14)	Chaplain attached to Royal Field Artillery, First World War
Bill Hayard (1919)	Bishop of St Asaph's and Bishop of St David's
John Stephens (1922)	Vicar of Bossall, near York
John Roberts (1927–29)	Minister of Otterburn, Northumberland
John Bartlett (1927–28)	Royal Navy chaplain
Tom Hollingdale (1927–30)	Vicar of St Peter's, Colchester

Note: Dates in brackets refer to Welsh international career.

— GRAND SLAM SPOILSPORTS —

Wales have spoilt the end of season Grand Slam parties planned by their opponents on six occasions. The Irish have suffered three times on Welsh soil, while the French were denied a possible first Grand Slam in Paris in 1955.

The game between Wales and France at Cardiff Arms Park in 1978 was the first time in Five Nations Championship history that both teams came into the last round of matches unbeaten and with the Slam at stake.

Date	Opponent (Venue)	Result	Captain
13th Mar 1926	Ireland (Swansea)	Won 11–8	Rowe Harding
10th Mar 1951	Ireland (Cardiff)	Drew 3–3	John Gwilliam
26th Mar 1955	France (Paris)	Won 16–11	Rees Stephens
8th Mar 1969	Ireland (Cardiff)	Won 24–11	Brian Price
18th Mar 1978	France (Cardiff)	Won 16–7	Phil Bennett
11th Apr 1999	England (Wembley)	Won 32–31	Rob Howley

— MEN OF THE DECADES, THE 1910s: BILLY TREW —

Billy Trew was the original utility player, a creative genius who played in all 12 Grand Slam games in 1908, 1909 and 1911 and earned a fourth Triple Crown in his first season of Test rugby. He ended with 29 caps over a record 14 seasons playing wing, centre and outside half and led his country 14 times.

Trew was a try scorer on his debut against England in 1900 at the age of 21 and picked up his first Triple Crown that season. It was the first of four seasons he played for Wales in which they never lost a championship match.

He played for Swansea, but not Wales, against the 1905 All Blacks, Glamorgan against the 1906 Springboks and then captained the 'All Whites' to victories over the 1908 Australians and the 1912 Springboks. A handy try scorer for club and country – he bagged 11 tries for Wales – his greatest ability was drawing attention to himself and creating time and space for others.

Having made his Swansea debut at 17 in October 1897, he helped the club become Welsh champions the next season, and for five of the following six seasons, and was the leading try scorer in Welsh club rugby in 1898/99 with 33 and 1899/00 with 31.

Injuries blighted his career between 1900 and 1902, but he hit back with 29 tries in 1903/04 and helped Swansea remain unbeaten in the 1904/05 campaign.

A boiler-maker by trade, he stood 5ft 8ins tall and weighed less than 11 stones. He soaked up punishment and always came back for more in more than 16 seasons of first-class action, six of which saw him captain the 'All Whites'.

He re-established himself in the Wales side in 1907 after missing the defeat by the Springboks. He led Wales for the first time in the 6–3 defeat in Scotland in what was Wales' last game with eight backs and seven forwards. But, having lost his first game as captain, he went on to win 12 of his next 13 in charge, including seven of the eight 1909 and 1911 Grand Slam games. Only the Newport forward Jim Webb was able to match his feat of playing in all 12 Grand Slam games in 1908, 1909, and 1911 and J.P.R. Williams and Gareth Edwards are the only other Welsh players who have since claimed three Grand Slams and played in all 12 games.

Trew scored four tries in the 1908 Grand Slam and five in 1909 while playing at centre, but controlled the 1911 campaign from outside half.

Highly principled off the field, he refused to play against Ireland in 1907 because he disagreed with a WRU suspension handed out to clubmate Fred Scrine for swearing at a referee.

He missed the game against England in 1912 because of injury, but still made a nuisance of himself by getting jailed for being drunk and disorderly in The Strand after the game.

He returned two weeks later for the 21–6 rout of Scotland at St Helen's, but then decided to tour Devon with his club instead of appearing in the last two championship matches.

His last two caps came at the age of 33 as captain in 1913 in the away wins over Scotland and France, but a groin injury then put paid to one of the greatest of all careers.

He went on to become a WRU selector, but died at the early age of 48. His son, Billy Trew junior, also captained Swansea and his son-in-law, Tom Day, played for Swansea and Wales.

— WELSH RUGBY'S NAME GAME —

The Joneses lead the way with the number of players and caps (see *Keeping Up With The Joneses*, page 72), but the Davieses lead the way in the captaincy stakes with 17 wins by eight Welsh skippers in 28 Tests.

Name	No	Caps	Captains	Matches	W	D	L
Jones	74	635	10	32	10	2	20
Davies	59	512	8	28	17	0	11
Williams	51	593	6	20	9	1	10
Evans	50	311	2	29	13	0	16
Thomas	40	487	6	36	17	1	18
Morgan	23	202	3	9	7	1	1
Rees	21	122	2	4	1	1	2
Lewis	19	157	3	8	3	0	5
Jenkins	14	263	1	2	0	0	2

— SIX OFF —

The final of the Godfrey Jones Cup in 1926 was supposed to be a grand affair. The competition had been started the previous season 'to improve Welsh rugby via the running game' and was played for among the Monmouthshire Union clubs.

But in the 1926 final the referee had to send off six players before Blaenavon beat Cross Keys 6–5.

— WALES' RECORD IN THE 1910s —

Played 22 Won 15 Drew 0 Lost 7
Tries: 69–28
Win percentage: 68.18%
Grand Slam/Triple Crown in 1911
Outright Championship win in 1911
Most appearances: Harry Uzzell (Newport) 11
Most tries: Reggie Gibbs (Cardiff) 10
Most points: Jack Bancroft (Swansea) 66
Most games as captain: Billy Trew (Swansea) 8
Most individual wins: Billy Trew (Swansea) 9

— CAP THAT LOT —

Steve Hansen selected the most experienced Welsh starting XV of all time when he sent out a team to face Italy at the Millennium Stadium on 27th March 2004 boasting 544 caps. It was his last game in charge as Wales coach and the team responded with Wales' biggest championship win for 94 years, 44–10.

It was a day to remember for lock Gareth Llewellyn as he won his record equalling 87th cap to join Neil Jenkins at the top of the Welsh cap list.

No	Name	Caps
15	Gareth Thomas	76
14	Rhys Williams	36
13	Mark Taylor	46
12	Iestyn Harris	24
11	Shane Williams	17
10	Stephen Jones	39
9	Gareth Cooper	19
1	Duncan Jones	9
2	Robin McBryde	32
3	Gethin Jenkins	18
4	Gareth Llewellyn	86
5	Michael Owen	12
6	Colin Charvis (capt)	67
7	Martyn Williams	44
8	Dafydd Jones	19

— TRY SCORING FULL BACKS —

Viv Jenkins became the first Wales full back to score a try in an international in the 13–0 win over Ireland at St Helen's, Swansea on 10th March 1934. It was to be another 33 years before another Welsh full back crossed an opponents' line – Keith Jarrett against England at the Arms Park in 1967.

In total, there have been 19 Welsh full backs who have scored Test tries. Kevin Morgan leads the way with 11, having scored five tries in four successive matches in 2005.

Wales' try scoring full backs (three or more tries)	
Kevin Morgan	11
JPR Williams	6
Shane Howarth	4
Gareth Thomas	4
Rhys Williams	4
Bryon Hayward	3 (as replacement)

— THE AUSTRALIAN CONNECTION —

James Bevan, the first Welsh captain, was born in Melbourne, Australia and became the first Welsh international on the register because there were no other players with surnames starting with 'A' or 'B'.

Bevan played only once for Wales in the massacre at Mr Richardson's Field, Blackheath, against England on 19th February 1881. His unique position as Wales' first captain was honoured 126 years later when his name was given to a trophy to be played for between Wales and Australia. The 'James Bevan Trophy' was won by the Wallabies in the two Tests in the summer of 2007 when it was first played for.

Other Australian-born Welshmen include Mapson Williams, Max Wiltshire, Gwilym Wilkins, Jason Jones-Hughes and Brent Cockbain.

— LEST WE FORGET: THE FIRST WORLD WAR —

The two Great Wars took a terrible toll on life and hundreds of Welsh rugby players were lost to the game. Of Wales' international cast, 16 capped players fell during the two World Wars. The unlucky 13 in the First World War were as follows:

- **Charles Taylor** was the first Welsh international to be killed in action. An engineer/captain of the 1st Battle Cruiser Squadron, he was killed aboard HMS Tiger at the Battle of Dogger Bank on 24th January 1915.
- **Billy Geen** followed his uncle, Frank Purdon, into both the Newport and Wales XVs. He was 24 when he met his death at Ypres on 31st July 1915 while fighting with the King's Royal Rifle Corps. His death was recorded as follows: "Geen fought gloriously, and was last seen alive leading his platoon in a charge after being for hours subjected to liquid fire."
- **Richard Williams** won his only cap in the first Welsh team against England in 1881. Born in Llowes, Radnorshire, he was a soldier before the outbreak of war, rising to the rank of major in the 1st Battalion, Royal Fusiliers. He retired at the age of 34 before rejoining at the age of 58 in 1914. He became a Lieutenant Colonel in the 12th Battalion, Royal Fusiliers and was killed in action at Loos on 27th September 1915.
- **Lou Phillips** formed a great half-back partnership for Newport and Wales with Llewellyn Lloyd and they helped Wales win the Triple Crown in 1900. When war broke out he refused a commission and enlisted in the Royal Welch Fusiliers. He became a sergeant and was killed in action at Cambrai on 14th March 1916, aged 38.
- **Dick Thomas, Johnnie Williams and Charlie Pritchard** all lost their lives in the space of 37 days on the Somme. Thomas and Williams made their Welsh debuts against the 1906 Springboks in a game in which Pritchard also figured. Thomas started life as a collier before joining Glamorgan Police. He became a company sergeant major in the Welch Regiment and was killed when leading a bayonet charge with the 16th Battalion in the first attack at Mametz Wood on 7th July 1916, aged 32.

  Williams equalled the Welsh try scoring record with 17 touchdowns in a 17-cap career that saw him help Wales win Grand Slams in 1908, 1909 and 1911. He notched 150 tries in

199 appearances for his home town club Cardiff and he captained both club and country. He was a captain in the Welch regiment and was fatally wounded in an attack at Mametz Wood and died on 12th July 1916, aged 34.

Pritchard was one of the heroes of the Welsh pack when they beat New Zealand 3–0 in 1905 and had helped Wales win the Triple Crown earlier in the year. Captain of his hometown club, Newport, from 1906–11, he was a captain in the 12th Battalion South Wales Borderers when he died on the Western Front. He was mentioned in dispatches for his bravery under fire as he led his men on a daring raid into enemy territory. Sent to take prisoners from the German trenches, Pritchard was shot twice as he led the raid. In a letter to his widow his commanding officer wrote: "He died as he would have wished, a truly glorious death, fighting for his country in a great cause. It was not given to all of us to die in such a haze of glory."

As he lay dying at No 1 Casualty Clearing Station Pritchard asked one final question: "Have they got the Hun?" When told the prisoner was safe he replied, "Well, I've done my bit." He was 33.

- **Horace Thomas** was a choral scholar at Cambridge University when he won his two caps in the 1912/13 season. He was a Temporary 2nd Lieutenant with the 11th Battalion, Rifle Brigade on the Somme at the time of his death. He was killed in action on 3rd September 1916 at the age of 26.
- **Brin Lewis** played for Swansea after leaving Cambridge University and won his two caps from there. He was a member of the Glamorgan Yeomanry who rose to the rank of major in the Royal Field Artillery before he was killed in action at Ypres on 2nd April 1917. He was 26.
- **Dai Westacott** was the Cardiff forward who was kicked so hard by his Australian opponent Albert Burge that the tourist was sent off by referee Gil Evans. That happened in Cardiff's victory over the Aussies in 1908 – two years after Grangetown-born Dai had won his sole cap against Ireland. A private in the Gloucestershire Regiment, he was killed in action in France on 28th August 1917. He was 35.
- **Phil Waller** was born in Bath, but became a Newport legend. He won six caps for Wales and three for the British Lions in South Africa in 1910. He never lost in a Welsh shirt and was in

WALES SHIRTS
1878–2009

1878-1881 South Wales

1881 v England

1900-1949

1949-1965

1965-1993

1987 World Cup

1993-95

1995 World Cup

1995 World Cup

1997

1997-2001

1999 World Cup

2001-03

2003 World Cup

2003 World Cup

2003-04

2005

2005 v France

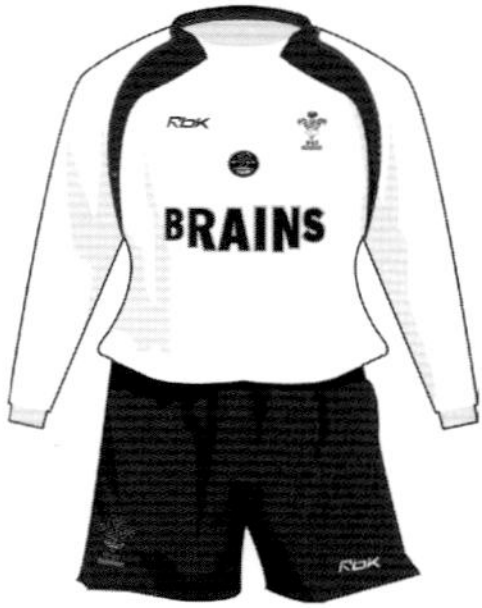

2005

2005
(WRU125th anniversary)

2006

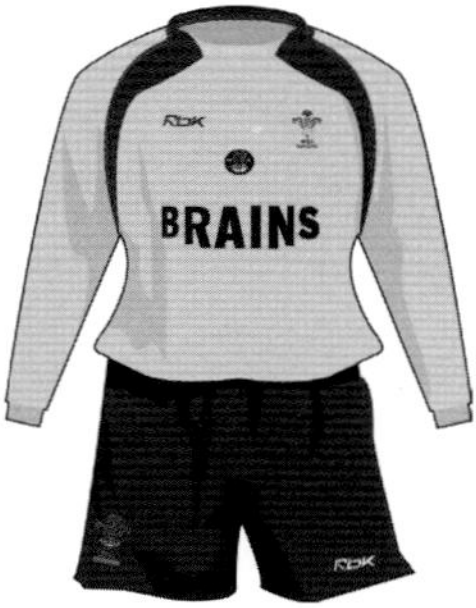

2006

2007 World Cup

2007 World Cup

WWW.CAKEBREADILLUSTRATIONS.COM

the pack that completed the Grand Slam in 1909. After the Lions tour he settled in South Africa, but enlisted in the South African Heavy Artillery Regiment at the outbreak of war. He rose to the rank of second lieutenant and was killed by shellfire in Arras on 14th December 1917. He was 28.

- **Fred Perrett** was born in Briton Ferry and played for both Aberavon and Neath. He won five caps for Wales before joining Leeds RLFC for a fee of £100 in 1913. At the outbreak of war he joined the Royal Welch Fusiliers and was a second lieutenant in the 17th Battalion when he was badly injured in battle in France. He died of his wounds, aged 27, after Armistice Day on 1st December 1918.

— CLOSED DOWN —

The WRU stepped in and shut down the Treorchy club on 12th October 1912, following a particularly violent match at their ground against Pontypridd. The Neath referee, Albert Freethy, and a number of Pontypridd players were assaulted by spectators and the ground was put off limits by the Union until 30th November.

How ironic, then, that the first game played on the ground after the ban was against Glamorgan Police on 5th December. The Chief Constable, his assistant and a number of local dignitaries attended the game, won 6–0 by the Police.

— WALES' RECORD IN THE 1920s —

Played 42 Won 17 Drew 3 Lost 22
Tries: 87–85
Win percentage: 42.5%
Outright Championship win in 1922
Most appearances: Steve Morris (Cross Keys) 19
Most tries: Rowe Harding (Swansea) 5
Most points: Albert Jenkins (Llanelli) 44
Most games as captain: Tom Parker (Swansea) 7
Most individual wins: Tom Parker (Swansea), Steve Morris (Cross Keys) 9

— MEN OF THE DECADE, THE 1920s: THE PARKER BROTHERS —

Wales played 42 matches in the twenties and won 17 times. On ten of those occasions one of the Parker brothers from Swansea, Tom and Dai, were in the Welsh pack.

Tom was born first, on 29th March 1891, and won the first of his 15 caps against the New Zealand Army team in 1919. Dai, 13 years younger, was born on 8th August 1904, and won the first of his ten caps just over a year after Tom had left the Test scene.

Both men captained Swansea – Tom in 1920/21 and Dai in 1927/28 – and Tom had the distinction of leading Wales seven times and never losing.

If the 1920s ranks among the worst decades for Welsh rugby success, the Parkers stand out like beacons for their drive and commitment. Tom helped Wales share the championship with England in 1920 and then led his side to the title in 1922, when only a draw in Scotland stopped Wales from completing the Grand Slam.

Tom was handed the Welsh captaincy a month before his 30th birthday against France at the Arms Park in 1921. Wales ended a run of two defeats as they won 12–4 to set up a run of six games without defeat under the Swansea man.

The Irish were seen off in Belfast in the final championship outing and then the 1922 campaign got off to a flying start with a 28–6 win over England in Cardiff. It was the biggest win over England since 1907 and Tom was one of eight try scorers as the Grand Slam champions of the previous season were put to the sword and lost their first championship game in eight games.

The next game in Scotland was a close run affair with the home side seemingly heading for victory until Islwyn Evans dropped a goal on the stroke of time to force a 9–9 draw. The Irish were beaten 11–5 at St Helen's before Wales' first outright championship title since 1911 was secured with a 11–3 win in Paris.

The captaincy was handed to Clem Lewis at the start of the 1923 championship. Wales lost to England and Scotland and the selectors – the 13 District Representatives on the WRU all had a hand in the process this season – turned to Tom once again to steady the ship.

Wales duly beat the French 16–8 on Tom's home town ground of St Helen's and he was able to bow out of international rugby with six wins and a draw as Welsh captain and eight wins and a draw in 15 Tests.

Dai made his Welsh debut in a 10–13 defeat by the Irish in Cardiff on 8th March 1924. He played seven games on the trot in 1924–25, enjoying wins over France in both Paris and Cardiff.

A useful place kicker, he kicked Swansea's only points against New Zealand in 1924 and was the Welsh place kicker against Scotland and France in 1925. He missed the next three seasons before reappearing in the final two championship matches of 1929, when Wales again beat France in Cardiff and drew with the Irish in Belfast. His final Welsh appearance was against England in Cardiff at the start of the 1930 championship, but that wasn't the end of his Test career. He went with the British Lions to New Zealand and Australia later that year and played in all five Tests.

— ROYAL COMMAND AT THE ARMS PARK —

Edward, Prince of Wales, became the first member of the Royal family to watch a Welsh international in Wales. On 8th March 1924 the prince, who was to become King Edward VIII, was joined by the Duke of York among a crowd of 35,000 who saw Ireland win 13–10 to earn their first victory in Cardiff for 25 years. He returned for the game against Scotland at the Arms Park on 5th February 1927, but once again Wales slumped to defeat, 5–0.

Prince Philip was at the Arms Park to open the Empire and Commonwealth Games in 1958, receiving his opening speech from the great Ken Jones as the final message relay runner. He was accompanied by the Queen in the WRU's Centenary season, 1980/81, when they came to see the combined England and Wales XV beat the combined Scotland and Ireland XV.

The Queen, who is the WRU's patron, presented the William Webb Ellis trophy to Aussie skipper John Eales when the Wallabies beat France in the 1999 Rugby World Cup final at the Millennium Stadium.

The current Prince of Wales, Charles, paid the first of his three visits to the ground in 1969 when he saw Wales beat Ireland 24–11. He also attended the Principality Cup final in 1992 and was at the Millennium Stadium in 2005 to join in the Grand Slam party.

Prince William, the new Vice Royal Patron, came with his mother, Princess Diana, to one game in the 1990s and was at the Wales v Ireland game in 2007 in his new capacity as Vice Royal Patron.

Diana came to four matches in the 1990s, including Wales' victory over England in 1993.

— THE ROUGHEST EVER —

The night before an international is supposed to be a time for gathering your thoughts, not picking your fights. But when players from the Irish and Welsh sides that were due to clash in Belfast on 14th March, 1914, met up at the theatre on the eve of the last official international before the First World War the friction began.

Skippered by Llanelli prop the Rev Alban Davies, the Welsh pack of 1914 built-up a fearsome reputation that led to them being known as "The Terrible Eight".

The sledging began when Irish pack leader Dr William Tyrrell told Uzzell that he was ready "to have a go" at Percy Jones the next day. Jones viewed it as more of a challenge than a threat. This is how he explained what happened as a result:

"We had an early warning of the rough house that was in store for us on the Friday night before the game when we went to the theatre and sat next to some of the Irish forwards," Jones, the great Newport and Pontypool forward recalled years later.

""Soon Dr Tyrrell came across and asked Harry Uzzell, 'Where's this Percy Jones you've got with you? I'll have a go at him tomorrow'.

"I replied, 'All right, I'm a Welshman, and I'll be with you'. Tyrrell added: 'Now, Jones, it's you and me for it tomorrow'."

That is how one of fiercest games of all time began. The next day at a rain soaked Balmoral ground Tyrrell was quick to score early points against Jones, but the personal feud soon turned into a no holds barred, general free for all.

"We didn't have to wait long before the fireworks started. Tyrrell got me in the first few minutes and everything inside my head rattled," recalled Jones.

"The next thing that happened was that their centre Myles Abraham kept having a go at me as well. So I called Uzzell over and said 'you'd better come with me'.

"After that we kept together and the fun went merrily on. At half-time Tyrrell's estimate of the score was that he was two up, and I agreed. But I promised him he wouldn't be leading for long.

"We decided it was time to get a move on and Uzzell, who was our pack leader, decided that we should play them at their own game. And we did!

"The play that followed was easily the fiercest that I ever saw or took part in – it waxed hotter and hotter, with no squealing by us or them, and after the game we were all the best of pals.

"Even Tyrrell gave in at last. 'You're the best Welshman I've ever run across, you are the only man who ever beat me'.

"The fiercest game that any of the 30 players had ever taken part in was followed by the friendliest dinner. Tyrrell and I sat together, and we signed each other's menu cards as a more permanent memento of the terrific struggle than the many bruises we had previously accepted from each other."

Wales won 11–3 and Tyrell never forgot the occasion. Later, as Sir William Tyrrell and President of the Irish Rugby Union, he invited Jones to be his personal guest at an Ireland v Wales game.

— BROKEN BUT UNBOWED —

In 1931, Wales beat Scotland 13–8 at the Arms Park with three tries – including one from pack leader Watcyn Thomas. Nothing odd about that except Thomas had earlier fractured his collarbone but refused to leave the field.

Thomas was only following the trend set by Dick Hellings some three decades earlier. The Llwynypia forward was a try scorer in the 13–3 victory over England at Gloucester in 1900 despite playing throughout almost the entire match with a fractured forearm.

— HACKED OFF —

New Zealand did their traditional Haka before the 2006 match against Wales at the Millennium Stadium in the privacy of their own changing room.

The pre-match Maori throwing down of the gauntlet is usually the aperitif adored by the crowd before the business begins. But the All Blacks took exception to news that Wales were planning to have the last word before kick-off with 'Hen Wlad fy Nhadau' following the Haka.

WRU officials claimed they were merely following a tradition that was started at the first meeting of the two nations back in 1905, when the Welsh anthem was sung after the Haka, but the All Blacks were singularly unimpressed. They retreated to their changing room and performed the Haka in front of a single television camera. New Zealand won the game comfortably.

— DUAL INTERNATIONALS —

To some die-hards it was tantamount to rape and pillage. For others the route 'north' seemed paved with gold. More than 160 Welsh internationals, one in four from every team selected between 1881and1995, turned professional.

What is more, some clubs found themselves completely ravaged by the northern raiders. Pontypool lost eight players one season to rugby league, while some villages lost almost a whole generation of men folk.

Some of the greatest names in British rugby league learned their trade at Welsh rugby clubs. Many represented their country before joining the paid ranks. David Watkins, Jonathan Davies and David Young hold the distinction of captaining Wales in both Union and League.

Out of the 91 in total, here is a list of the ten most-capped players who have played for Wales in both codes:

Name	**Last RU club**	**First RL club**	**Move**	**Caps**
Scott Quinnell *	Llanelli	Wigan	1994	52 + 2
Scott Gibbs *	Swansea	St Helens	1994	53 + 3
David Young *	Cardiff	Leeds	1990	51 + 13
Allan Bateman * ^ #	Neath	Warrington	1990	35 + 12
Jonathan Davies ^ #	Llanelli	Widnes	1989	32 + 9
Steve Fenwick *	Bridgend	Cardiff Dragons	1981	30 + 2
Adrian Hadley	Cardiff	Salford	1988	27 + 9
Iestyn Harris ^ #	Cardiff Blues	Warrington	2001	25 + 15
Rob Ackerman *	Cardiff	Whitehaven	1986	22 + 5
David Watkins * ^ #	Newport	Salford	1967	21 + 16

* Rugby Union Test Lions
^ Rugby League Lions tourist
# GB rugby league cap

— ENGLAND OR WALES? —

Ernest Dyer Galbraith Hammett holds the unique distinction of playing for both Wales and England at international level, his remarkable double career including playing amateur football for Wales against England and rugby for England against Wales.

Born in Radstock, Somerset, he played all his rugby in Newport. But before he made the highest grade in rugby, Hammett became an international on the soccer pitch. Playing for Treharris in the Welsh League, the 20-year-old won a Wales Amateur cap against England on 17th February 1912.

England won that game 3–0 in Bishop Auckland and Hammett didn't appear again in the Welsh line-up. He moved on to play for Newport County before concentrating on rugby with Pill Harriers and then Newport.

Pill were a major force in south Wales around the time of the First World War and went unbeaten during the 1918/19 season, winning 30 of their 32 games and drawing the other two. Hammett joined forces with Jerry Shea at centre and the two men became vital for the 'Whites' and then the 'Black and Ambers'. One of those two draws was against the New Zealand Army 'B' team – their top side were playing Australia at Bradford in the King's Cup – when 10,000 fans crammed in to witness a 0–0 game.

Both Hammett and Shea were Newport players when the 1919/20 season kicked off and formed a brilliant centre combination. The Welsh selectors stuck with the multi-talented Shea as their choice for the midfield and invited Hammett to team up with him in red for the championship opener against England at St Helen's on 17th January, 1920.

The only problem was that Hammett had been invited to play for England in the same fixture the day before. He had accepted and couldn't go back on his word. On the face of it he made the wrong decision. Shea became the first player in history to go through the scoring card as he scored 16 points in a 19–5 Welsh triumph.

But Hammett had the last laugh. He went on to win eight caps for England and helped them to win the Grand Slam in 1921, beating Wales, Shea included, 18–3 at Twickenham.

— WELSH RUGBY FIRSTS 2 —

The first Wales cap to die was Samuel Goldsworthy on 28th September 1889, in Swansea at the age of 34.

The first Welsh win over England on English soil came on 15th February 1890 at Crown Flat, Dewsbury. Wales won by a try from Buller Stadden to nil.

Wales lost all three matches in a season for the first time following defeat to Ireland on 5th March 1892. The next occasion would not be until 1923.

Wales' first victory in Scotland came on 4th February 1893 at Raeburn Place, Edinburgh, when Wales scored their first tries in Scotland and won 9–0.

The first victory over England in Wales came on 7th January 1893 at Cardiff Arms Park when Wales won 12–11.

The first Welsh Triple Crown was secured at Stradey Park on 11th March 1893, when Ireland were beaten 2–0.

The first hat-trick of tries for Wales was scored by Willie Llewellyn on his debut against England at St Helen's on 7th January 1899. Llewellyn became the first player to score four tries on debut for any country.

The first Welshman to captain a British Lions team was Teddy Morgan. He led the Lions to a 17–3 victory over Australia in Brisbane on 23rd July 1904. He also captained the side in two further Tests.

The first game against New Zealand took place at Cardiff Arms Park on 16th December 1905, when Wales won 3–0.

The first touring side to score against Wales was South Africa, who won 11–0 at St Helen's on 1st December 1906. Neither the 1888 Maoris, nor the 1905 All Blacks scored a single point

Wales' first game against France was at Cardiff Arms Park on 2nd March 1908, when Wales won 36–4.

Wales became the first team to beat England, Scotland, Ireland and France in the same season in 1908.

The first game against Australia was at Cardiff Arms Park on 12th December 1908 when Wales won 9–6.

The first game in France was at the Stade Colombes on 23rd February 1909, when Wales won 47–5.

Charles Gerald Taylor was the first Wales international player to be killed in the First World War. He was serving on HMS Tiger on the Dogger Bank when struck by gunfire on 24th January 1915.

The first Welsh player to go through the scoring card was Jerry Shea, who scored a try, conversion, penalty and two drop goals against England at St Helen's on 17th January 1920.

The first Welsh full back to score a try was Viv Jenkins against Ireland on 10th March 1934.

The first international to be televised live came on 19th December 1953, when Wales beat New Zealand 13–8 at Cardiff Arms Park.

Australia beat Wales for the first time on 3rd December 1966 at the Arms Park. The tourists triumphed 14–11 in a game that saw debuts for Wales from Barry John, Gerald Davies and Delme Thomas.

France won their first Grand Slam in Cardiff when they beat Wales 14–9 on 23rd March 1968.

The first Home International to be fully sponsored was on 5th February 1983, when Wales met England at Cardiff Arms Park in the British Gas Challenge.

The first international to be televised live came on 19th December 1953, when Wales beat New Zealand 13–8 at Cardiff Arms Park.

— TAKING IT ALL —

Neil Jenkins has bagged the three biggest solo points efforts by a Welsh player scoring all his country's points in a game. He kicked all 24 points in the 26–24 defeat by Canada at the Arms Park in 1993 and grabbed all 18 in the victory over Tonga in 1994. He also scored all 17 points in Dublin in 1994 when Wales won 17–15. Meanwhile, Paul Thorburn kicked 15 points in a 23–15 defeat by the French in Cardiff in 1986.

Highest scorers of all Wales' points in a game:

Pts	Name	Date	Opponent (Venue)	Result
24	Neil Jenkins	10th Nov 1993	Canada (Cardiff)	Lost 24–26
18	Neil Jenkins	22nd Jun 1994	Tonga (Nuku'alofa)	Won 18–9
17	Neil Jenkins	5th Feb 1994	Ireland (Dublin)	Won 17–15
15	Paul Thorburn	1 Mar 1986	France (Cardiff)	Lost 15–23

Highest scorers of all a country's points in a game against Wales:

Pts	Name	Date	Team (Venue)	Result
21	Rob Andrew	18th Jan 1986	for England (Twickenham)	Lost 18–21
21	Matt Burke	25th Nov 2001	for Australia (Cardiff)	Lost 13–21
21	Chris Paterson	10th Feb 2007	for Scotland (Murrayfield)	Lost 9–21
19	Dusty Hare	17th Jan 1981	for England (Cardiff)	Won 21–19
18	Gonzalo Quesada	1st Oct 1999	for Argentina (Cardiff)	Won 23–18

— MEN OF THE DECADES, THE 1930s: CLAUDE DAVEY —

You only had to ask the Bath and England centre Ron Gerrard about the strength and power of Claude Davey. Gerrard temporarily lost the sight in one eye at Twickenham in 1933 after being on the receiving end of one of the Garnant-born midfield powerhouse's hand-offs.

Davey was the first 'battering ram' to add a touch of steel to the Welsh midfield. The crash tackler on who the great Jack Matthews based his game, he also had style and panache to back up his brawn. According to the legendary Wales full back, Viv Jenkins, Davey "had the smile of an angel, but tackled like an avenging Fury."

Capped by the Welsh Secondary Schools in 1927, he graduated to one of the highest honours in the Welsh game – captaining a team that beat New Zealand. By the time he scored one of Wales' three tries in their 13–12 victory over the 1935 All Blacks on 21st December he had already tasted victory against them for Swansea three months earlier.

That game had been less of a close run thing as the All Whites, inspired by the schoolboy half backs Willie Davies and Haydn Tanner, won 11–3. Davey ran in two of the three home tries, one from 35 yards.

Davey also scored the first try of the Test match – one of five for Wales – and marshalled his men as New Zealand fought back to lead 12–10 with six minutes to play. Wales were down to 14 men after Don Tarr had been forced off the field with a broken neck, but Davey kept his side going. A crowd of more than 50,000 held their breath as Wilf Wooller chipped the All Blacks defence and the wing, Geoffrey Rees-Jones, pounced on it to score the winning try. The crowd invaded the pitch to carry off their conquering heroes, and the All Blacks captain Jack Manchester admitted: "I've never played in such a thrilling game."

Davey was a well-travelled rugby player in the 1920s and 1930s, turning out for Swansea, Sale, Cwmgors, Amman United, Aylesbury, Reading, London Welsh, Rosslyn Park, Berkshire, Lancashire and the Barbarians. He won 23 caps in all and captained his country eight times.

His international career began against France at Stade Colombes on 21st April 1930. Wales won 11–0 in a match Davey later described as "the roughest of my career". Of his 23 caps, he was on the losing side only seven times and of his eight games as captain, he lost only two.

He played throughout the Welsh championship winning season of 1931 and was captain against Scotland in the 1936 team that also won the title outright. He was also in the first Welsh side to win at Twickenham, 7–3, in 1933. Davey was one of only two players who survived the 'clean-out' at the end of the 1933 season, when selectors handed out an incredible 13 new caps for the opening match of the 1934 season against England in Cardiff.

Last word on the great man goes to his Swansea and Wales team-mate, Tanner: "In many ways, he was quite underrated, but for those who played alongside him, he was a truly inspirational captain and colleague."

— CHARVIS' YELLOW FEVER —

The only Wales player to have been sent to the sin-bin four times in his career is Colin Charvis – against France at Stade de France on 29th March 2003, Canada in Melbourne during the 2003 Rugby World Cup and in successive games against Argentina at Tucuman and Buenos Aires on 12th and 19th June 2006.

Wales' first recipient of a yellow card was Rob Appleyard handed out by referee Ed Morrison against Ireland at Lansdowne Road on 21st March 1998, although in those days the yellow card meant a formal caution and not a spell in the sin-bin.

Scott Quinnell wrote his name into the record books when he became the first Welshman, and the first player in the Five/Six Nations championship, to be given a 10–minute cooling off period when he was sent to the sin-bin by English official Chris White in the 43rd minute of the game against France at the Millennium Stadium on 5th February 2000.

James Griffiths was the first Welshman to pick up a yellow card on debut, doing so in the 57th minute against Samoa in Cardiff on 11th November 2000.

— WALES' RECORD IN THE 1930s —

Played 34 Won 18 Drew 3 Lost 13
Tries: 55–39
Win percentage: 52.94%
Outright Championship wins in 1931, 1936
Beat New Zealand 1935 (13–12)
Most appearances: Claude Davey (Swansea) 23
Most tries: Wilf Wooller (Cardiff) 6
Most points: Viv Jenkins (Bridgend) 35
Most games as captain: Jack Bassett (Penarth) 9
Most individual wins: Claude Davey (Swansea) 14

— BOKS BEATEN . . . AT LAST —

After trying and failing 12 times, it was unlucky 13 for South Africa as Wales at last beat the Boks in the opening game at the Millennium Stadium on Saturday 26 June 1999. The first match played at the new ground had a restricted crowd of 27,500 as the final touches were being put to the stadium ahead of the 1999 Rugby World Cup finals.

But the few witnessed history as Wales triumphed 29–19 with Neil Jenkins scoring the first points at the new home of Welsh rugby and centre Mark Taylor taking the honours of scoring the first try.

— LIKE FATHER, LIKE SON —

Fathers and sons who have played for Wales:

Father	**Caps**	**Son(s)**	**Caps**
Tom Baker Jones (1882–85)	6	Paul 'Baker' Jones (1921)	1
Howell Jones (1904)	1	Elwyn 'Howie' Jones (1930)	2
George Travers (1903–11)	25	'Bunner' Travers (1937–49)	12
Glyn Stephens (1912–19)	10	Rees Stephens (1947–57)	32
Jack Gore (1924–25)	4	Billy Gore (1947)	3
Windsor Lewis (1926–28)	6	Geoff Windsor Lewis (1960)	2
Idwal Davies (1939)	1	Brian Davies (1962–63)	3
Len Blyth (1951–52)	4	Roger Blyth (1974–80)	6
Jim Shanklin (1970–73)	4	Tom Shanklin (2001-current)	42
Derek Quinnell (1972–80)	23	Scott Quinnell (1993–99)	52
		Craig Quinnell (1995–99)	

In addition to this list, George Vickery was capped for England from Aberavon in 1905. His son, Walter was capped for Wales from Aberavon in 1938/39 (see *Family Feud*, page 19). Dai Hiddlestone won five caps from Neath between 1922–24 and his grandson, Llanelli's Terry Price, won eight caps between 1965–67.

— JONATHAN GETS THE DROP ON THE REST —

Jonathan Davies: 13 drop goals for Wales

Jonathan Davies got the drop on the rest of Wales' kickers when he overtook Barry John's drop goal record of eight.

Coming on as a replacement for Malcolm Dacey in the Rugby World Cup clash with Tonga in Palmerston North on 29th May 1987 Davies fired over his ninth goal. He had already dropped two goals in the opening victory over Ireland in Wellington to set a tournament record and eventually took his Welsh tally to 13 in 32 Tests.

Neil Jenkins holds the record for the most drop goals in a match by a Welshman – three against Scotland at Murrayfield in 2001. The first drop goal recorded for Wales in an international came from the boot of Buller Stadden on his debut in the victory over Ireland at the Arms Park on 12th April 1884.

The first forward to bag a drop goal for Wales was Martyn Williams at the 2003 Rugby World Cup. Having come on as a replacement in Canberra against Tonga he dropped a goal to help Wales win 27–20.

Leading drop goal scorers for Wales:

Name	Career	Caps	Drops
Jonathan Davies	1985–1997	28+4	13
Neil Jenkins	1991–2002	81+6	10
Barry John	1966–1972	25	8
Gareth Davies	1978–1985	21	7

— THE FLYING MINERS —

When Wales played against Scotland at Murrayfield in 1934 they were followed by their usual army of fans. But one group failed to make it to Edinburgh.

Eight miners from Tylorstown decided to charter a special plane, adorned with the Prince of Wales feathers, a leek and a daffodil, and headed north. Or at least that's what they thought. A problem working out the compass meant they ended up watching a soccer match in Portsmouth instead.

Undaunted, 'the flying miners', as they became known, headed to Belfast the following season and successfully joined 10,000 other Welsh fans at Ravenhill to see Wales lose 9–3 to Ireland.

— TWICKENHAM SOUVENIR —

So relieved were the Welsh fans at seeing Terry Davies' penalty soar over the crossbar to force a draw with England at Twickenham in 1958, that a few of them decided to take a souvenir. Led by Fred Mathias, a top Welsh jockey from Manorbier, a group climbed back into the ground after dark and sawed down the crossbar at the north end.

They cut it into three, 3ft pieces to take back with them to Pembrokeshire the next day. Stopping for a cup of tea in a Cotswolds café on the Sunday they were delighted when Davies came in behind them and agreed to sign their prized souvenirs.

The attitude at Twickenham by this time was not, however, quite as favourable. Nothing like this had ever happened before at 'HQ' and an investigation was begun. As it happened, Davies was a timber merchant and offered to replace the crossbar himself. However, Mathias owned up and wrote a letter of apology to the Secretary of the RFU, Colonel Doug Prentice.

The cross bar can still be found in pride of place in a pub in Manorbier.

— KEEPING UP WITH THE JONESES —

The Jones clan entered the Guinness Book of Records in 2006 when 1,224 met up in Cardiff to overtake the 583 Norbergs who had gathered in Sweden to break the previous record.

In rugby terms, Harlequins prop Ceri Jones became the 74th Jones (excluding Hugh Williams-Jones, Jason Jones-Hughes and Tommy Jones-Davies) to be capped by Wales when he came on as a replacement against Australia in the first Test in the summer of 2007. It meant the Joneses extended their lead over the Davieses by 15 players and 118 caps.

The biggest gathering of Joneses in a Wales XV is six. This has happened on two occasions up to the summer of 2007 – against South Africa in Cardiff in 2004 and Scotland in Edinburgh in 2007.

6 Nov 2004	**10 Feb 2007**
Wales v South Africa (Cardiff)	Scotland v Wales (Murrayfield)
Lost 36–38 Lost 9–21	
15 Gareth Thomas (capt)	15 Kevin Morgan
14 Hal Luscombe	**14 Mark Jones**
13 Sonny Parker	13 Jamie Robinson
12 Gavin Henson	12 James Hook
11 Shane Williams	11 Chris Czekaj
10 Stephen Jones	**10 Stephen Jones** (capt)
9 Dwayne Peel	9 Dwayne Peel
1 Duncan Jones	**1 Duncan Jones**
2 Steve Jones	2 Rhys Thomas
3 Adam Jones	**3 Adam Jones**
4 Brent Cockbain	4 Robert Sidoli
5 Michael Owen	**5 Alun Wyn Jones**
6 Dafydd Jones	6 Alix Popham
7 Colin Charvis	7 Martyn Williams
8 Ryan Jones	**8 Ryan Jones**

— 50 UP —

Gareth Edwards was the first Welsh player to reach 50 caps. Having made his debut against France in Paris on 1st April, 1967, he reached the milestone on 4th February, 1978. His 50th consecutive Test came at Twickenham at the start of Wales' grand Slam season. It was to be his last season in the game, his third Grand Slam, and he was 30.

Only one other player in the history of international rugby has ever won his first 50 caps in successive matches – All Black full-back Christian Cullen, between1996 and 2000.

It took legendary scrum half Edwards almost 11 years to reach his half-century, while Llanelli Scarlets No 9 Dwayne Peel became the 17th player to reach the mark against Scotland in the 2007 RBS Six Nations campaign. Peel was the youngest Welsh player to reach 50 caps, aged only 25, and he achieved it in less than six years.

Six of the '50 Club' are forwards and four of them are scrum halves.

Welsh rugby's 50 caps club (as of July 1st 2007):

Caps	Starts/reps		
96	(92+4)	Gareth Thomas	(1995–2007)*
92	(82+10)	Gareth Llewellyn	(1989–2004)
87	(81+6)	Neil Jenkins	(1991–2002)
88	(80+8)	Colin Charvis	(1996–2007)*
72	(72)	Ieuan Evans	(1987–1998)
71	(61+10)	Martyn Williams	(1996–2007)*
62	(55+7)	Stephen Jones	(1998–2007)*
59	(58+1)	Rob Howley	(1996–2002)
58	(51+7)	Garin Jenkins	(1991–2002)
55	(55)	J.P.R. Williams	(1969–1981)
54	(53+1)	Robert Jones	(1986–1995)
53	(53)	Gareth Edwards	(1967–1978)
53	(53)	Scott Gibbs	(1991–2001)
54	(35+19)	Dwayne Peel	(2001–2007)*
52	(50+2)	Scott Quinnell	(1993–2002)
52	(49+3)	Mark Taylor	(1998–2006)
51	(47+4)	David Young	(1987–2001)

* Current internationals

— QUICK OUT OF THE BLOCKS —

Who is the fastest player to have played for Wales? Here are a few contenders:

Arthur Gould: Midland Counties 110 yards and 120 yards hurdles champion in 1892, he won £1,000 in foot races.
Rowe Harding: Welsh 100 yards champion in 1922 and 1926, he had a championship best of 10.4 seconds. He also won the Welsh 220 yards title in 1923 in 23.9 seconds and was second in 1926.
Ronnie Boon: Welsh 220 yards champion in 1929 in 23.4 seconds, he was second in 1931.
Jack Matthews: Welsh junior 220 yards champion in 1937 in 24.0 seconds and second in 1939 100 yards senior championships.
Keith Maddocks: Welsh junior 100 yards champion in 1944 in 10.8 seconds
Ken Jones: Olympic semi-finalist over 100 metres in 1948 and a silver medallist in the relay. Shared Welsh 100 yards record from 1948–59 with 9.8 seconds and clocked a hand-timed 10.6 seconds at the Olympics.
Gareth Griffiths: Welsh junior 100 yards champion in 1950 in 10.4 seconds.
Dewi Bebb: Finished second in Welsh 100 yards final in 1961 in 9.8 seconds and third over 220 yards in 22.5 seconds.
Bill Morris: Finished third in Welsh 220 yards final in 1962 in 22.2 seconds.
Keri Jones: Finished second in Welsh 220 yards final in 1966 in 21.8 seconds. Reached second round of 100 and 220 yards at Commonwealth Games. Helped the Welsh relay team to finish fourth in Welsh record time of 40.2 seconds that stood for 30 years.
J.J. Williams: Did Welsh sprint double in 1971 in 10.8 and 21.7 seconds. Ran windy times of 10.6 seconds and 21.4 seconds at the 1970 Commonwealth Games. Best times of 10.5 seconds legal and 10.4 wind assisted over 100 metres.
Arthur Emyr: Finished third in the Welsh 100 metres final in 1988 in 11.0 seconds
Richard Wintle: Welsh 200 metre champion in 1985 in 22.6 seconds.
Nigel Walker: Welsh champion at 100 metres twice, 200 metres once and 110 hurdles three times. AAA hurdles champion, finalist at Commonwealth Games and European Championships, semi-finalist at Olympic Games and indoor bronze medallist at World and European championships. With a 100 metre best time of 10.47 seconds and 10.35 seconds wind assisted, is among the quickest players ever to have played the game.

— FIRST IN THE AIR —

Lewis Jones set many records in his glittering rugby union and league careers, one of which will never be broken. One of the odd men out of the 1950 Wales Grand Slam team not selected for the British Lions tour to Australasia that summer, he eventually got the call to replace the injured Irish full back George Norton.

It was a request that led to an amazing four and a half day journey from London to Gisborne, in New Zealand. While the rest of the Lions had taken three weeks to sail to New Zealand, the teenage Jones became the first Lion to fly.

It was to be an epic journey for the man who had marked his debut on the international stage in the Five Nations Championship as an 18-year-old a few months earlier by helping Wales to win at Twickenham for the first time in 17 years and then go on to notch their first Grand Slam since 1911.

"I was playing cricket in Plymouth for one of the Services teams when I got the call to go to New Zealand. I was fielding in the covers when someone ran onto the field and said there was an urgent phone call for me," recalled Jones.

"I was a Rating in the Royal Navy doing my National Service and I loved playing cricket. In fact, I played at Lord's for the Navy against the Army and the RAF.

"When I got to the phone it was a Mr Haig-Smith who informed me that George Norton had broken his arm in New Zealand and that the Lions intended to send out a replacement.

"He asked me if I would like to go. I had just turned 19 and was only just getting over the disappointment of being one of only two players who had played throughout the Welsh Grand Slam season who had not been picked to tour.

"My first thought was about what I would tell the Navy, but he assured me he would fix that. Within a week everything had been fixed for me to fly out to New Zealand to join the tour. No Lion had ever flown before, but they worked out a schedule for me to go by air.

"I'd never been on a plane before, but I had a journey to the other side of the world to look forward to. I went from my home in Swansea to London Airport and boarded a Boeing Stratocruiser.

"Up it went and, within half-an hour, down it came again – in Shannon. Next stop was Newfoundland and then New York. There was a change of planes in New York, a Super Constellation aircraft, and on to Chicago and then San Francisco, where I had to stay the night.

"That's where I ran into a bit of a problem. I was only allowed to take £25 transit money with me and I'd used some of it in New York. When I arrived in San Francisco I took a taxi into town to find a hotel.

"By the time I got there I'd used all my money on the cab fare. I spent the night and left rather quickly in the morning without paying. I went to the nearest travel agency, explained my dilemma and they arranged to put me on an airport bus.

"I was glad to be back in the air, on another Super Constellation, and the first stop in the Pacific was Canton Island. It was so small I think the only thing on the island was the landing strip and refuelling truck. Honolulu was next on the agenda before I flew to Sydney.

"There was another change of plane in Sydney as I headed to Auckland, and then another change of aircraft to take me to finally team up with the Lions in Gisborne.

"When I arrived, after four and a half days of travelling, Bleddyn Williams was there to meet me. Two days later I was making my Lions debut against Poverty Bay, East Coast and Bay of Plenty."

Jones played in 11 games, made three Test teams and was second highest scorer on the tour with 92 even though he missed the first 12 of the 29 matches.

And the trip home? "It was a three-week boat trip stopping in Ceylon and coming via the Suez Canal – it was fantastic," said Jones.

— WALES' RECORD IN THE 1940s —

Played 13 Won 6 Drew 1 Lost 6
Tries: 18–11
Win percentage: 46.15%
Beat Australia 1947 (6–0)
Most appearances: Ken Jones (Newport) 13
Most tries: Ken Jones (Newport) 5
Most points: Bill Tamplin (Cardiff) 24
Most games as captain: Haydn Tanner (Cardiff) 12
Most individual wins: Ken Jones (Newport), Gwynfor Evans (Cardiff), Bleddyn Williams (Cardiff) 6

— ALL FOUR THREE-QUARTERS —

Wales have taken the field with a three-quarter line from the same club on eight occasions. Three clubs have provided the bulk of the back division – Cardiff on the first six occasions, Bridgend and Llanelli.

The first time was against Ireland on 10th March 1894 when the Cardiff quartet of Norman Biggs, Dai Fitzgerald, Jack Elliot and Tom Pearson took the field for Wales in a 0–3 defeat.

In the 1911 Grand Slam season, Wales won using the same three-quarter line, again from Cardiff, in three of the four matches. Between them, Reggie Gibbs, Louis Dyke, Billy Spiller and Johnnie Williams played together four times for Wales and were winners on every occasion.

Louis Dyke made his debut in their first appearance together in the win over Ireland in Dublin in 1910, but missed the opening match of the 1911 Grand Slam campaign against England – a 15–11 win in Swansea. In their four games together Wales scored 19 tries and the Cardiff three-quarters grabbed 14 of them.

One club three-quarter lines:

10th March 1894	Ireland 3, Wales 0	Belfast

Cardiff: Norman Biggs, Dai Fitzgerald, Jack Elliot, Tom Pearson

12th March 1910	Ireland 3, Wales 19	Dublin
4th February 1911	Scotland 10, Wales 32	Inverleith
28th February 1911	France 0, Wales 15	Paris
11th March 1911	Wales 16, Ireland 0	Cardiff

Cardiff: Reggie Gibbs, Louis Dyke, Billy Spiller, Johnnie Williams

1st February 1930	Scotland 12, Wales 9	Murrayfield

Cardiff: Gwyn Davies, Lou Turnbull, Graham Jones, Ronnie Boon

10th December 1988	Wales 9, Romania 15	Cardiff

Bridgend: Glen Webbe, Mike Hall, John Devereux, Richard Diplock

18th June 1994	Fiji 8, Wales 23	Suva

Llanelli: Ieuan Evans, Neil Boobyer, Nigel Davies, Wayne Proctor

— MEN OF THE DECADES, THE 1940s: KEN JONES —

Welsh rugby star and Olympic medalist

The problem with Ken Jones is deciding what he is most famous for. Is it the try that won the 1953 game for Wales against New Zealand; his near length of the field epic for the British Lions in New Zealand in 1950; his Welsh, and world record cap tally of 44; his Welsh record equalling 17 tries, or his tally of eight tries in Wales' Grand Slam successes of 1950 and 1952?

It is a tough call, although the great man himself always held his achievements of the summer of 1948 closest to his heart. That was the year the Olympic Games were staged in London and Ken was presented with a gold medal at Wembley. For as well as being one of the greatest wings the game of rugby has ever seen, the

Blaenavon-born flyer was also one of Wales' greatest athletes. He won 17 domestic sprint titles and set four sprints records.

Before he won the first of his 44 caps, 43 of which were in succession, against England in Cardiff on 18th January 1947, he had already become All-India Olympic Games 100 yards champion and begun his domination of the Welsh AAA 100 and 200 metre crowns. He did the sprint double for the first time in 1946 and won them every year up to 1954 – except when he was on duty with the Lions in New Zealand and Australia in the summer of 1950.

Three victories in 1946 got Jones selected for the British athletics team to run in Oslo and Helsinki and he was on track for the London Olympics. Then, at the Southern Counties championships in 1948, he equalled the English native and Welsh national 100 yards records with a time of 9.8 seconds.

"When I think back on my career as both a rugby player and an athlete I'd have to pick the 1948 Olympic Games as the highlight. The atmosphere at Wembley was electric and it was a bit scary initially," recalled Jones. "Reaching the semi-finals of the 100 metres, and being among the 12 fastest men in the world, as well as winning the silver medal in the relay, has to top the lot."

Jones anchored the British quartet, which included English rugby international Jack Gregory, to second place in the final. Their time of 41.3 seconds kept them six yards behind the Americans, who took the tape in 40.6 seconds, and ahead of Italy and Hungary.

But then the Americans were disqualified and Jones, Gregory, McDonald-Bailey and McCorquodale were called out to podium to receive the gold medals. The following morning the Americans won their appeal against a faulty change-over and the British heroes were forced to go back to Wembley from their Uxbridge camp and hand back their medals. "It took almost a month for us to have our silver medals sent to us," said Jones.

Wales played 13 games in the 1940s and Jones was the only player to feature in every one of them. He scored two tries against Scotland in Edinburgh in his second appearance and helped Wales share the Five Nations title with England in his first season.

He scored 145 tries in 293 matches for Newport and went on to captain Wales once. He was also made captain of the British athletics team at the 1954 European Championships, where he again struck silver in the sprint relay, and he claimed a bronze for Wales over 200 metres at the Empire and Commonwealth Games in Vancouver in the same year.

— CARDIFF RULE —

On 17th January 1948 at Twickenham, Cardiff provided ten players to the Wales team to face England. It is a record that still stands 60 years on for a Welsh starting XV.

The side was also skippered by a Cardiff player, Haydn Tanner. They were unable to combine to beat England though, the game ending in a 3–3 draw.

The Welsh selectors kept faith with the same ten players for the next two Championship matches – a 14–0 win over Scotland in Cardiff and an 11–3 defeat at Swansea to France.

Counting replacement appearances, the Ospreys also contributed ten players – seven starters and three substitutes – in the 10–45 defeat to New Zealand at the Millennium Stadium on 25th November 2006.

ENGLAND v WALES, 1948

Full-back	**Frank Trott**	**Cardiff**
Wing	Ken Jones	Newport
Centre	**Bleddyn Williams**	**Cardiff**
Centre	**Billy Cleaver**	**Cardiff**
Wing	**Jack Matthews**	**Cardiff**
Outside-half	Glyn Davies	Pontypridd
Scrum-half	**Haydn Tanner**	**Cardiff (capt)**
Prop	Les Anthony	Neath
Hooker	**Mal James**	**Cardiff**
Prop	**Cliff Davies**	**Cardiff**
Lock	Des Jones	Llanelli
Lock	**Bill Tamplin**	**Cardiff**
Flanker	Ossie Williams	Llanelli
Flanker	**Gwyn Evans**	**Cardiff**
No 8	**Les Manfield**	**Cardiff**

— SMALLPOX STOPS PLAY —

An outbreak of smallpox in the Rhondda forced the championship match between Ireland and Wales, scheduled to be played in March 1962, to be postponed by eight months.

It was eventually played at Lansdowne Road, Dublin, on 17th November. The game ended in a 3–3 draw.

— WHAT A GIVE AWAY —

The greatest lead Wales have built up in a Test only to lose the game is 17 points, 'achieved' twice.

The first was at Cardiff on 25th September 1996 in a friendly against France. Wales, and Barry Williams in particular, had made a great start, the Neath hooker scoring a try within two minutes of the start on his debut. By the half-time break the lead was 17 points at 27–10. After the break the French tore into their hosts with a try from Jean-Luc Sadourny and the unerring boot of Richard Dourthe. With five minutes to go Dourthe's conversion of Abdelatif Benazzi's try had levelled the scores at 33 apiece. However, two minutes later Les Bleus completed a remarkable rearguard action when centre Stephane Glas went over – and Dourthe's fourth conversion took him to 20 points on the night and France had won 40–33.

This unfortunate 'feat' was then equalled in Sydney on 26th May 2007, when Wales piled up a 17–0 lead after just 20 minutes. By half-time Australia had eaten into the advantage and were only trailing 12–17. The Wallabies then hit the front for the first time on 62 minutes with a Stirling Mortlock penalty. Ten minutes later James Hook nosed Wales back in front at 23–22 with a smartly taken drop goal. But heartbreak was to come when replacement No 8 Stephen Hoiles crashed over in the corner after the full-time hooter had sounded to snatch the very latest of victories for the Wallabies.

— WORLD CUP FEVER —

Wales may still be dreaming of Rugby World Cup success in the union code, but former Neath forward John Thorley got his hands on the most precious silverware in the game when he helped Great Britain win the inaugural Rugby League World Cup in 1954.

Great Britain, led by the former Scottish union international Dave Valentine, beat France 16–12 in the final at Parc des Princes in front of 37,000 fans. Welsh skipper Will Banks was also in the squad that played four games to win the World Cup, while Billy Boston and Tommy Harris were in the 1960 squad that regained the title from the 1957 winners, Australia.

The last time there was a British winner in the Rugby League World Cup, in 1972, the GB captain was Cardiff-born Clive Sullivan.

— LEST WE FORGET: SECOND WORLD WAR —

The toll on Welsh rugby's internationals in the Second World War, at least in terms of loss of life, was not as harsh as in the previous global battle. There were three fatalities – Cecil Davies, John Evans and Maurice Turnbull.

- **Cecil Davies** was born in Pontypridd and won one cap against England in 1934 while playing for the RAF and London Welsh. He became the RAF heavyweight boxing champion in 1932 when he beat the Irish international George Beamish in the final. He was killed in action on Christmas Day, 1941, at the age of 32.
- **John Evans** won his single cap in the same pack as Davies against England on the day the new North Stand was opened at Cardiff Arms Park. To make it an even more special occasion the Newport hooker was made captain. He had played for Wales Schools at Under-15 and Secondary Schools levels before playing for his home town club 190 times, including against the 1935 All Blacks. A lieutenant in the 3rd Battalion of the Parachute Regiment, he was killed in action in North Africa on 8th March 1943 at the age of 31.
- **Maurice Turnbull** was one of the greatest all-round sportsmen ever produced by Wales. He played cricket for England, rugby (two caps) and hockey (three caps) for Wales and was the Welsh squash champion. A Major in the 1st Battalion Welch Guards, he was killed in action on 5th August 1944, when leading a group of men on a raid on a column of Panzer tanks in Montchamp.

— EVERYTHING OVERBOARD —

As the Welsh team travelled back from Belfast having secured the Triple Crown with a 6–3 triumph in March 1950, the celebrations got a little out of hand on the ferry crossing home. In a cabin belonging to one of the four Cardiff players in the victorious side a party developed that involved pork pies and a large number of bottles of Guinness. The cabin owner left for a short while and in his absence the revellers decided to throw everything they could lay their hands on through the port-hole and out to sea – mattress included.

When the ferry docked at Heysham nobody was allowed ashore until two detectives had interviewed the chief suspects and some red faced WRU officials. In the end, the WRU Secretary Eric Evans had to pay £80 compensation to get the Welsh party off the boat.

— A WELSH RUGBY/CRICKET XI —

1. Hugh Morris: Outside half for South Glamorgan Institute, Aberavon and Newport, he captained Glamorgan and went on to open for England for three Tests. One of Glamorgan's greatest run scorers, he won the championship and One Day titles. He scored 19,785 first class runs.

2. Gilbert Parkhouse: The Swansea full-back was coached in both sports by Billy Bancroft. He played against the Kiwis for the All Whites in 1945 and for England in seven Tests between1950–59. Scored 22,619 runs in 435 games for Glamorgan.

3. Tony Lewis: A double Cambridge Blue, he played full back for Neath and Gloucester. He played 315 games for Glamorgan, was captain for six seasons and led them to the championship in 1969. He played nine times for England and captained them on their tour to India and Pakistan. He topped 15,000 runs for Glamorgan.

4. Willie Jones: Captained Neath in 1938/39 and played for Wales against England in a Red Cross wartime international in 1940. Also played for Neath against the Kiwis in 1945. In 340 games for Glamorgan he reached 1,000 runs in a season seven times. Hit two double centuries in the 1948 championship-winning season and scored more than 13,000 runs.

5. Alan Rees: Won three caps while with Maesteg in 1962 before joining Leeds RL. Scored 7,681 runs in 216 games for Glamorgan.

6. Maurice Turnbull: Was a Test cricketer between 1930–36, winning nine caps, and an international rugby player on two occasions in 1933. He ended up playing 314 games for Glamorgan and scoring 14,431 runs, captaining the team for nine summers.

7. Wilf Wooller: He won 18 caps for Wales, including a debut win at Twickenham in Wales' first triumph there and victory over the 1935 All Blacks, and was captain of Glamorgan from 1947–60. Played 400 games for the county scoring 12,692 runs and taking 882 wickets.

8. Billy Bancroft: Played 33 consecutive times for Wales and was captain of the 1900 Triple Crown team. Scored more than 8,000 runs for Glamorgan as an all-rounder.

9. Viv Jenkins: Played 14 times for Wales and became the first full back to score a try. A double Blue at Oxford, he played 44 times for Glamorgan between 1931–37 as a wicketkeeper/batsman and scored 1,072 runs.

10. Selwyn Biggs: Won nine Welsh caps and played with Bancroft in the 1900 Triple Crown victory in Belfast. Was a pacy opening bowler for Glamorgan, taking 116 wickets.

11. Austin Matthews: Played rugby for Penarth, East Midlands and Northampton, whom he captained, and had a final Welsh trial. Made one Test appearance for England against New Zealand in 1937 and took 227 wickets for Glamorgan. He also played table tennis for Wales.

— ARMS PARK DREAM TEAM —

Ever wondered what the dream team would be at Cardiff Arms Park? Of the 695 Welsh caps who played in the 174 internationals between1884–1997, when the ground was turned through 90 degrees to create the magnificent Millennium Stadium, here is the team with the most successful win ratio.

The most successful Welsh players at Cardiff Arms Park:

	P	W	D	L	Tries	Win Ratio
15 JPR Williams	29	24	2	3	2	83%
14 Gerald Davies	22	18	1	3	13	82%
13 Ray Gravell	12	10	0	2	1	83%
12 Steve Fenwick	15	13	0	2	2	87%
11 JJ Williams	15	13	1	1	9	87%
10 Phil Bennett	17	14	2	1	2	82%
9 Gareth Edwards	28	23	2	3	12	82%
1 Ray Prosser	13	9	0	4	0	69%
2 Bobby Windsor	14	12	1	1	1	87%
3 Graham Price	22	18	1	3	1	82%
4 Geoff Wheel	16	15	0	1	0	94%
5 Allan Martin	18	16	0	2	1	89%
6 Jeff Squire	15	12	1	2	1	80%
7 Clem Thomas	10	8	0	2	0	80%
8 Mervyn Davies	20	17	2	1	0	85%

Note: To qualify for this list, players must have played at least 10 matches.

— MEN OF THE DECADE, THE 1950s: BLEDDYN WILLIAMS —

It was Wales international Wilf Wooller who recommended Bleddyn Williams for a sporting scholarship at Rydal. It was a long way from his Taffs Well home, but the north Wales school helped to turn another great talent into a sporting giant.

Bleddyn made his Cardiff debut for the Athletic XV at the age of 16 years and 47 days in the 1938/39 season. It was also the first season that Wooller led the Blue and Blacks. Playing at centre alongside his brother, Brinley, he couldn't stop Cardiff losing 14–8 away from home to Ebbw Vale.

By the time he retired in 1955 Williams had made 283 first team appearances, scored 283 tries, including a record 41 in one season, led his club to victory over the 1953 All Blacks and also played in a winning side over Australia. Injuries prevented him from winning more than 22 caps for Wales, although he did lead his nation to its last victory over New Zealand in 1953 to make it a club and country double.

He was set to captain Wales in 1950, but withdrew with a knee injury. Wales won the Grand Slam that season and Williams only figured in three of the next 13 Tests, which included only one appearance in the 1952 Grand Slam campaign, due to injury and illness. He re-appeared in the 1953 championship and took over the captaincy from John Gwilliam after the home defeat to England. He won all his five games as Wales skipper and also led the 1950 British and Irish Lions in two of their six Tests in New Zealand and Australia.

Williams played in three Services and seven Victory internationals, but didn't earn his first Welsh cap until he was almost 23. He had joined the RAF as a 20-year-old and, after training near Phoenix in Arizona, went on to rise to the rank of flight lieutenant, flying gliders in behind enemy lines. His most dangerous trip came the week before he was due to play for the British Army against the Dominions at Leicester. Having hit his target and landed safely in Germany the last thing on his mind was playing rugby.

"We dropped over the Rhine the weekend before the game and, on the Friday, I was still in Germany, having spent six nights sleeping in a slit trench with only an American parachute for cover," recalled Williams. "On that Friday the major in charge, Hugh Bartlett – who captained the Sussex cricket team – asked me if I was playing the next day. When I said I had a fat chance of that he said 'pack your bags because you are off.'

"He drove me to the Rhine, which I crossed on a barge, and then on to the base in Eindoven. From Holland I was flown to Brize Norton where my CO picked me up and flew me back to base camp at Rivenhall, where I arrived around midnight. We made it to Leicester by lunchtime. I scored a try and Great Britain won the match."

It was one of many tries for the man who inherited Gwyn Nicholls' title as the 'Prince of Wales centres'.

— WALES' RECORD IN THE THE 1950s —

Played 43 Won 29 Drew 2 Lost 12
Tries: 68–39
Win percentage: 67.44%
Grand Slams/Triple Crowns in 1950 and 1952
Outright Championship wins in 1950, 1952, 1956
Beat New Zealand in 1953 (13–8) and Australia in 1958 (9–3)
Most appearances: Ken Jones (Newport) 31
Most tries: Ken Jones (Newport) 12
Most points: Terry Davies (Llanelli) 44
Most games as captain: John Gwilliam (Edinburgh Wands/Gloucester) 13
Most individual wins: Ken Jones (Newport) 22

— STRADEY OR NOT? —

The first Welsh international match played in Llanelli was against England on 8th January 1887. But while the game was scheduled for Stradey Park, the traditional home of Llanelli rugby club, the contest had to be transferred to the cricket pitch adjoining the rugby ground because of the frozen state of the pitch.

The English players refused to play on the Stradey pitch, but agreed to go ahead with the game on the cricket field. The only problem was that the grandstand was facing the rugby ground and so those spectators who had purchased tickets had to stand on the makeshift touchlines.

— WILLIE'S RECORD BREAKING START —

Six days after his 21st birthday Willie Llewellyn wrote his name into the record books with four tries on his Welsh debut in the record-breaking 26–3 win over England at St Helen's, Swansea on 7th January 1899.

First capped while with his native Llwynypia club, Llewellyn became the toast of the nation as he ran in a record four tries against the old enemy. Not only was it the first hat-trick scored by a Welshman, but in more than 500 games since then no player has been able to better the feat.

His try in the defeat to Scotland in his next game enabled him to overtake Arthur Gould as Wales' leading try scorer and, when he scored his ninth international try against Scotland at the Arms Park on 1st February 1902, he took the world record for Test tries.

Llewellyn hoisted his world record mark to 16 in 20 games between1899 and 1905 and was much revered in his local community. Having returned from London as a pharmacist, he set up shop in Tonypandy. During the 'Tonypandy Riots' in 1910 more than 60 shops were damaged but Llewellyn's remained untouched.

His Welsh and world try records fell to Cardiff wing Johnny Williams in 1911 when he crossed for his 17th try in the Grand Slam season. England wing Cyril Lowe moved the record to 18 and beyond on 10th February 1923.

— DEATH UNDERGROUND —

Swansea scrum-half Tudor Williams holds the unenviable record of being the youngest Welsh rugby international to die. Williams, who won his only cap in the victory over France in Cardiff in 1921, lost his life when he was electrocuted while working at the Blaencaegurwen Colliery in July 1922. He was 23.

Other Welsh internationals who lost their lives in coal industry related accidents include Penarth's Dickie Garrett, who was crushed at Penarth Docks in 1908 when a truck ran over him when he was working as a tipper for the Taff Vale Railway Company.

Newport's Harry Jarman died from pneumonia at the age of 45 after being injured at a mine when he threw himself in front of a runaway truck that was heading for some children.

Cliff Richards, who won five caps from Pontypool in the 1920s, worked underground all his life before finally perishing there at the age of 62 in an accident at the Navigation Colliery, Crumlin in 1964.

— WHITEWASHES —

Wales suffered their first Five Nations Championship whitewash in the 1990 tournament, losing at home to France and Scotland and away against England and Ireland.

They also lost coach John Ryan in the process. Ryan resigned after the 34–6 defeat at Twickenham, which then represented Wales' heaviest Five Nations defeat. That season also saw lock Kevin Moseley banned for 32 weeks after being sent-off for stamping against France.

The second championship whitewash came five years later with Wales losing at home to England and Ireland and on the road to France and Scotland. And history repeated itself with another Welsh red card – prop John Davies against England – and the resignation of coach Alan Davies.

Both those whitewashes consisted of four defeats. But in 2003, Wales went one worse when they lost all five in the now Six Nations Championship.

It started with an unwanted 'first' – Italy beating Wales for the first time in Rome. From there it simply got worse and worse with England and Ireland winning at the Millennium Stadium and Wales going down away to Scotland and France. Quite simply, a year to forget.

— THE DASHING COOPER —

Abergavenny-born Fred Cooper was the first real flier in Welsh rugby. Having captained his home town club he moved to Newport in 1892. He played for three seasons with the Black and Ambers before turning professional with Bradford.

He scored eight tries in 20 games in his first season at Newport and went on to top the rugby league scoring charts in 1899/1900 with 39 goals. He was also the first Welshman to top 100 points in a season in rugby league.

But it was as a sprinter that Cooper probably made his biggest mark. He equalled the British record for 100 yards for the first time at the Welsh Championshps in 1898 and then became the first Welshman to win the AAA 100 yards at Stamford Bridge, London, in July that year, once again clocking 10 seconds. That time stood as a Welsh record for 36 years. During 1891 and 1892 he won £60 worth of prizes at meetings around south Wales.

No wonder he was often referred to as the fastest man ever on a rugby field.

— MEN OF THE DECADES, THE 1960s: CLIVE ROWLANDS —

Clive Rowlands became the first man to captain and coach a Wales team to a Triple Crown – and he did it within the space of five years.

'Top Cat' was a born leader – he captained the Welsh Schools team to South Africa in 1956 and later won 14 consecutive caps, skippering Wales on each occasion. He went on to reach the highest positions in the game – Wales and British Lions team manager and President of the Welsh Rugby Union – and was a man who was never lost for words. A great motivator, his team talk before matches in the seventies were the catalyst for many successes.

As manager of the Wales team at the inaugural Rugby World Cup in 1987 he was asked where Welsh rugby went after losing 49–6 to New Zealand in the semi-finals. "Back to beating England in Cardiff every other year," was his quick retort. Wales had beaten England in the quarter-finals and had remained unbeaten against the auld enemy in Cardiff since he had made his debut in 1963.

Rowlands had formed a new half-back partnership with David Watkins when he won his first cap against the English at the Arms Park on 19th January 1963. They played together 14 times. A canny tactician, his kicking skills became legendary after he was responsible for the majority of the 111 line-outs in the 6–0 win over Scotland at Murrayfield in 1963. It may not have been good to watch, but no Welsh fan was complaining while celebrating a first win in Edinburgh in 10 years.

Born in Upper Cwmtwrch on 14th May 1938, Clive was captain of Pontypool when he was called up to the Welsh team. He later switched to Swansea, where he was captain in 1967/68, before taking over as the Wales National Coach in succession to David Nash. Clive was a schoolmaster in his early years, having graduated from Cardiff Training College, and had all the attributes to become a good coach.

After a difficult first season in charge, Rowlands then masterminded five wins and two draws in his next eight championship matches as Wales shared the title with the Scots in 1964 and won it outright the next year.

He led Wales on their first overseas tour to South Africa in 1964, although the 24–3 Test defeat in Durban was the biggest in 40 years. In the wake of the tour the WRU set up an investigation into the state of the game and made recommendations that led to a National Coaching structure being created. The response from Rowlands and his team was to win the Triple Crown for the first time in 13 years in 1965.

Five months after hanging up his boots at the end of the 1967/68 season, Rowlands was assistant manager for the Wales tour to Argentina. In all but name he was coach for the two uncapped Tests.

So started one of the greatest coaching careers in Welsh rugby history. He blooded JPR Williams and Mervyn Davies in his first official international as Wales coach, against Scotland in 1969, and went through his first championship season unbeaten. The Triple Crown triumph over England in Cardiff in April featured four tries from Maurice Richards and Welsh rugby's second 'Golden Era' had commenced.

— WALES' RECORD IN THE 1960s —

Played 48 Won 20 Drew 6 Lost 22
Tries: 68–61
Win percentage: 41.67%
Triple Crowns in 1965, 1969
Outright Championship wins in 1965, 1966, 1969
Beat Australia in 1969 (19–16)
Most appearances: Brian Price (Newport) 32
Most tries: Dewi Bebb (Swansea) 10
Most points: Keith Jarrett (Newport) 73
Most games as captain: Clive Rowlands (Pontypool) 14
Most individual wins: Brian Price (Newport) 14

— NON-COUNTRIES —

As well as having given caps against 20 different countries up to the summer of 2007, Wales have also awarded Test status to games against six non-national teams.

Date	Opponent	Result	Venue
22nd Dec 1888	New Zealand Natives	Won 1G, 2T-0	Swansea
21st Apr 1919	New Zealand Army	Lost 3–6	Swansea
26th Nov 1927	New South Wales	Lost 8–18	Cardiff
6th Oct 1990	Barbarians	Lost 24–31	Cardiff
24th Aug 1996	Barbarians	Won 31–10	Cardiff
11th Nov 2006	Pacific Islands	Won 38–20	Cardiff

— SHEA'S FULL HOUSE —

Newport centre Jerry Shea was a real handful. A professional boxer, he was also a noted swimmer and a professional runner. He played four times for Wales before joining Wigan RL and winning two caps for the Welsh rugby league team.

Standing 5ft 6in tall, and weighing only 10st 7lbs, he beat Frank Moody, Gypsy Daniels and Johnny Basham in notable fights, but lost to the former world welterweight champion Ted 'Kid' Lewis.

He made his Welsh debut in the defeat by the New Zealand Army in 1919 before writing his name into the record books against England in his second outing at St Helen's in the first Championship match played after the First World War on 17th January 1920. Having opened the scoring with a penalty goal he then put Wales back in front with a dropped goal after Harold Day had scored a try for England. Then came an individual try at the posts which he also converted. A second dropped goal – then worth four points - brought him a 16 points haul in the match and helped Wales to a 19–5 victory at the start of a season in which they won the title outright.

Shea's achievement in going through the scoring card made him the first player in almost 50 years of Test rugby to complete every scoring feat in one game.

The next player to complete rugby's 'full house' was over 30 years later by Wales full back Lewis Jones playing for the British Lions against Australia on 19th August 1950.

— HOME HUMILIATION —

Wales suffered their first home defeat by a nation outside the traditional 'Big Eight' when Romania triumphed 15–9 at the Arms Park in 1988.

In the acrimonious fall-out of the defeat Jonathan Davies – who had captained the side – joined Widnes in a £200,000-plus deal less than a month later.

Three years later and there was more pain, when Western Samoa dumped Wales out of the 1991 World Cup in their own backyard with a 16–13 defeat. That defeat gave rise to the famous epitaph: "Thank goodness it wasn't the whole of Samoa".

— WALES TOUR CAPTAINS —

CAPPED TOURS

Year	Host nation	Captain	Club
1964	South Africa	Clive Rowlands	Pontypool
1969	New Zealand/Australia/Fiji	Brian Price	Newport
1978	Australia	Terry Cobner	Pontypool
1986	Tonga/Fiji/Samoa	David Pickering	Llanelli
1988	New Zealand	Bleddyn Bowen	SW Police
1990	Namibia	Kevin Phillips	Neath
1991	Australia	Paul Thorburn	Neath
1993	Namibia/Zimbabwe	Gareth Llewellyn	Neath
1994	Canada/Fiji/Tonga/Samoa	Ieuan Evans	Llanelli
1995	South Africa	Jonathan Humphreys	Cardiff
1996	Australia	Jonathan Humphreys	Cardiff
1997	USA/Canada	Gwyn Jones	Cardiff
1998	South Africa/Zimbabwe	Robert Howley	Cardiff
1999	Argentina	Robert Howley	Cardiff
2001	Japan	Andy P Moore	Swansea
2002	South Africa	Colin Charvis	Swansea
2003	Australia/New Zealand	Martyn Williams	Cardiff Blues
2004	Argentina/South Africa	Colin Charvis	Tarbes
2005	USA/Canada	Mark Taylor	Scarlets
2006	Argentina	Duncan Jones	Ospreys
2007	Australia	Gareth Thomas	Toulouse

WALES XV TOURS

1968	Argentina	John Dawes	London Welsh
1969	New Zealand/Australia/Fiji	Brian Price	Newport
1973	Canada	Gareth Edwards	Cardiff
1975	Hong Kong/Japan	Mervyn Davies	Swansea
1980	North America	Steve Fenwick	Bridgend

WALES B TOURS

1983	Spain	Eddie Butler	Pontypool
1989	Canada	Paul Thorburn	Neath

DEVELOPMENT TOUR

2000	Canada	Richard Smith	Ebbw Vale

— BROTHERLY LOVE —

From the Gwynns in the 1880s to the Brews in the 2000s, there have been 33 sets of brothers who have played for Wales.

David and William Gwynn, of Swansea, paved the way. David, first capped in 1882, won six caps and William, who made his debut in 1884, five. They never played together for Wales and so the honour of being the first brothers to play in the same Welsh team fell to Bob and Arthur Gould against England in 1885. Bob and Arthur played together five times for Wales, Bob being skipper on one occasion, while a third Gould, Bert, won three caps in 1892 and 93 in Welsh sides captained by Arthur. Only one other family has provided three sons to the Welsh team – the Jonses of Pontypool.

The Quinnell brothers, Scott and Craig, hold the record for the most games played together in a Wales shirt with 25 joint appearances.

Pre First World War	**Total caps**
David Gwynn (5), William Gwynn (6)	11
Bob Gould (11), Arthur Gould (27), Bert Gould (3)	41
George Harding (4), Charles Harding (3)	7
Evan James (4), David James (5)	9
David Sameul (2), John Samuel (1)	3
Charles Nicholl (15), David Nicholl (1)	6
Norman Biggs (8), Selwyn Biggs (9)	17
Sid Nicholls (4), Gwyn Nicholls (24)	28
Tom Dobson (4), George Dobson (1)	5
'Ponty' Jones (1), Jack Jones (14), Tuan Jones (1)	16
Billy Bancroft (33), Jack Bancroft (18)	51
Teddy Morgan (16), Willie L Morgan (1)	17
John Dyke (1, Louis Dyke (4)	5
Harry Wetter (2), Jack Wetter (10)	12
Inter-War Years	
Wickham Powell (4), Jack Powell (1)	5
Tom Parker (15), Dai Parker (10)	25
Bert Hollingdale (2), Tom Hollingdale (6)	8
Bobby Jones (3), Dick Jones (1)	4
John Roberts (13), William Roberts (1)	14
Bernard Turnbull (6), Maurice Turnbull (2)	8
Glyn Prosser (4), Dai Prosser (2)	6
Jack Bassett (15), Arthur Bassett (6)	21
Will James (2), Tommy James (2)	4
Harold W Thomas (6), David L Thomas (1)	7

Post Second World War

Terry Davies (21), Len Davies (3)	24
Bleddyn Williams (22), Lloyd Williams (13)	35
Richard Moriarty (22), Paul Moriarty (21)	43
Glyn Llewellyn (9), Gareth Llewellyn (92)	101
Gareth Williams (5), Owain Williams (1)	6
Scott Quinnell (52), Craig Quinnell (32)	84
Andrew P Moore (26), Stephen Moore (3)	29
Richard Wintle (1), Matthew Wintle (1)	2
Nathan Brew (1), Aled Brew (3)	4
Jamie Robinson (21), Nicky Robinson (12)	33

Note: Frank Hancock (1884–86) won four caps for Wales and his brother, Froude, was capped by England (1886–96) 3 times.

Martyn Jordan (1885–89) won three caps for Wales and his brother, Charles, was capped once by Ireland (1884).

Brent Cockbain (2003–07) has won 24 caps for Wales and his brother, Matt, played 63 times for Australia (1997–2003).

— WALES COACHES —

Name	Reign	Played	Won	Drawn	Lost
David Nash	(1967–68)	5	1	1	3
Clive Rowlands	(1968–74)	29	18	4	7
John Dawes	(1974–79)	24	18	0	6
John Lloyd	(1980–82)	14	6	0	8
John Bevan	(1982–85)	15	7	1	7
Tony Gray	(1985–88)	18	9	0	9
John Ryan	(1988–90)	9	2	0	7
Ron Waldron	(1990–91)	10	2	1	7
Alan Davies	(1991–95)	35	18	0	17
Alex Evans	(1995)	4	1	0	3
Kevin Bowring	(1995–98)	29	15	0	14
Dennis John	(1998)	2	1	0	1
Graham Henry	(1998–2002)	34	20	1	13
Lynn Howells	(2001)	2	2	0	0
Steve Hansen	(2002–04)	29	10	0	19
Mike Ruddock	(2004–6)	20	13	0	7
Scott Johnson	(2006)	3	0	1	2
Gareth Jenkins	(2006–)	15	4	1	10

— MEN OF THE DECADES, THE 1970s: GARETH EDWARDS —

Gareth Edwards: Nobody ever did it better – and maybe no one ever will!

It was all there for one of the greatest natural athletes ever produced by Wales from an early age. A centre for Welsh Secondary Schools, he had soccer trials with Wales Youth and was looked at by Swansea City scouts. The Welsh Games Committee named him as the 'Most Promising Athlete' of 1964 and he was the English Schools 200 yards hurdles champion.

Athletics and soccer's loss was rugby's gain. The youngster from Gwaun-cae-Gurwen, who used to practice his passing in the lane using a house brick, became arguably the world's greatest rugby player of all time.

An inaugural member of the International Rugby Hall of Fame, a member of the Welsh Sports Hall of Fame's 'Roll of Honour', the first Welsh Player of the Year and consistently voted in the greatest Welsh and British and Irish Lions XVs, Gareth Edwards was simply the best player of his era.

Why? Perhaps it was something to do with his explosive power, immense strength, fantastic skill or his ultra-competitiveness. Or maybe it was the fact he played a world record 53 consecutive internationals for Wales, becoming the first Welsh player to top 50 caps, or that he was the first choice on three successive Lions tours.

Edwards captained Wales 13 times, the first when he was only 20, and was in charge when Wales played their 100th Test at Cardiff Arms Park against Scotland on 19th January 1974. Wales won six and drew three of the games in which he was in charge and he lost only once as captain in Cardiff.

He scored a record 20 tries for Wales in full internationals and won three Grand Slams and five Triple Crowns.

Edwards enjoyed great success against the other leading rugby-playing nations but it was his clashes with New Zealand, and their dominant scrum half of the era, Sid Going, in particular, that defined him. He became the focal point of their defensive structure, the one threat they found hard to contain.

He never beat the All Blacks with Wales, losing in 1967 and 1973, but he drew against the 1967 tourists with East Wales and then helped the Barbarians defeat them so famously at the Arms Park in 1973. In tandem with his most famous half-back partner, Barry John, he helped guide the Lions to their only Test series victory to date in New Zealand in 1971. The Lions won two and drew one of the four Tests.

In 63 Tests with Wales and the Lions Edwards served only five outside halves. They were quite a cast – David Watkins (2), Mike Gibson (1), Barry John (28), John Bevan (4) and Phil Bennett (28 + 1). When he first met John ahead of a Welsh trial appearance the two men hit it off immediately.

"You throw it and I'll catch it," was the then Llanelli No 10's advice to his junior partner. They thrilled crowds around the world for Cardiff, Wales and the Lions.

Edwards' brilliance is as enduring as his achievements. He became MBE in 1984 and was made CBE in 2007.

'That try' for the Barbarians against the All Blacks in 1973 is the most played in the history of the game – scored at the opposite end of the Arms Park to his amazing 70-yard kick and chase score in the mud against the Scots a year earlier.

Nobody ever did it better – and maybe no one ever will!

— SPRINGBOK DEMOS —

When Dawie de Villiers brought his Springbok team to the UK and Ireland in 1969/70 there were Anti-Apartheid demonstrations almost everywhere they went. Among the most vociferous was at Swansea on 15th November 1969 at their fourth game.

Some of the most amazing scenes in the history of Welsh rugby occurred at St Helen's when 30–40 demonstrators burst onto the field and staged a sit-down protest shortly after half-time. There had been tension outside the ground before the game started, but when the demonstrators invaded the pitch they received short shrift. The police, joined by Swansea RFC 'stewards' cleared the spectators within five minutes to allow the game to continue.

There were many allegations of ill-treatment by the demonstrators, many of whom were women, against the Swansea 'stewards'. In the end, 200 demonstrators and 10 policemen were injured and there were many arrests.

The police conducted an investigation into the handling of the pitch invasion and exonerated their officers and the 'stewards'. But from there on, it was the police who dealt with all operations at matches. When the Springboks played Wales at the Arms Park, the pitch was ringed with barbed wire to ensure nobody got onto the pitch.

One of the leaders of the demonstrations was Peter Hain, who went on to become Secretary of State for Wales and MP for Neath.

— WALES' RECORD IN THE 1970s —

Played 46 Won 32 Drew 3 Lost 11
Tries: 104–41
Win percentage: 69.57%
Grand Slams/Triple Crowns in 1971, 1976, 1978
Other Triple Crowns 1977, 1979
Outright Championship wins in 1971, 1975, 1976, 1978, 1979
Beat Australia in 1973 (24–0) and 1975 (28–3) and drew with South Africa 1970 (6–6)
Most appearances: JPR Williams (London Welsh/Bridgend) 44
Most tries: Gareth Edwards (Cardiff) and Gerald Davies (London Welsh/Cardiff) 17
Most points: Phil Bennett (Llanelli) 166
Most games as captain: Gareth Edwards (Cardiff) 10
Most individual wins: JPR Williams (London Welsh/Bridgend) 32

— BRILLIANT BEN —

Ben Beynon was a remarkable ball player. A Welsh rugby international, he played professional soccer with Swansea Town before joining Oldham RLFC.

Beynon launched his Swansea rugby union career in 1913 and then played for Swansea Town as an amateur in the last competitive season before World War I took hold.

Still in his teens, Beynon's greatest moment on a football field came on 9 January, 1915, when he rifled home the winner for the Southern League Division 2 side against reigning English Champions Blackburn Rovers at The Vetch Field in the First Round of the FA Cup.

The Swans' 1–0 victory sent shock waves around the country and remains one of the biggest upsets in the history of the FA Cup. In the next round he helped the Swans force extra-time at First Division Newcastle United before the game ended in a 1–1 draw.

In the replay in Swansea, the Geordies proved too strong and ended Beynon's cup dreams with a 2–0 win. There was more cup heartache at the end of the season when Wrexham beat Swansea 1–0 in the Welsh Cup Final at Ninian Park. Beynon scored the goal in a 1–1 draw in the first game at The Racecourse, but couldn't find the net in the replay.

After the First World War, Beynon was selected to play for Wales in the first championship game in six years and played at scrum half in a 19–5 win over England at St Helen's when he became the 300th Welsh rugby international.

He kept his place for the next game in Scotland before stunning the sporting world by signing professional terms with Swansea Town in the Southern league First Division.

A week after playing scrum half for Wales in the 9–5 defeat at Inverleith he was at centre forward for the Swans against Queens Park Rangers. The WRU instantly professionalised him and withheld his cap as a result.

Beynon scored 11 goals in 26 league outings and netted a hat-trick against

Norwich in September, 1920.

Beynon switched codes again in 1922 when he joined Oldham RLFC. He played 94 games over four seasons, scoring 77 points, and figured in the 1925 Challenge Cup final victory over Hull KR at Headingley.

In 1926 he returned to soccer with Swansea Town, although he didn't add to his league appearances with the club.

— RED MIST SHAME —

Geoff Wheel made an unwanted triple first against Ireland at the Arms Park in 1977 when he was sent off by Scottish referee Norman Sanson.

The giant Swansea lock became the first Welshman to be issued with his marching orders in an international match, the first international player to be sent off in Wales and the first player to be dismissed in a Five Nations match. The only consolation for Wheel was that Sanson also gave Irish No 8 Willie Duggan an early bath at the same time after he had caught the two players exchanging blows at a line-out.

Technically, the first international player to be actually shown a red card in a Test match was Wales prop John Davies, as the practice of brandishing coloured cards was introduced into Test match rugby in 1995.

The complete record of Welsh dismissals is:

Player	Min	Opponents	Date	Referee
Geoff Wheel	38	v Ireland (Cardiff)	15th Jan 77	Norman Sanson (Sco)
Paul Ringer	13	v England (Twickenham)	16th Feb 80	David Burnett (Ire)
Huw Richards*	77	v New Zealand (Brisbane)	14th Jun 87	Kerry Fitzgerald (Aus)
Kevin Moseley	32	v France (Cardiff)	20th Jan 90	Fred Howard (Eng)
John Davies	62	v England (Cardiff)	18th Feb 95	Didier Mene (Fr)
Garin Jenkins	75	v S Africa (Jo'burg)	2nd Sep 95	Joel Dume (Fr)

*Richards was the first player in Rugby World Cup history to be dismissed during the 1987 semi-final match

— FORTRESS ARMS PARK —

Wales were unbeaten at home in the Five Nations championship for 27 straight Tests between their 14–9 defeat by France in 1968 and their 34–18 mauling by Scotland in 1982.

The following season the match against Scotland was again significant – Wales winning 19–15 at Murrayfield to end a seven-match losing run away from home.

— ONE CAP WONDERS 2 —

Another selection of players who pulled on the famous red shirt on just the one occasion:

- **John Evans** was only the third player to captain Wales on his debut when he led Wales against England at the Arms Park on 20th January 1934. The Newport hooker was one of 13 new caps in the side – and one of five players discarded after a 9–0 defeat.
- **George Parsons** became the youngest second row to play for Wales when he made his debut against England at the Arms Park in 1947 at the age of 20 as one of 13 new caps in the first post-WWII championship match. The Newport was picked to play in France but as the team travelled by train to London he was ordered home on the suspicion of negotiating with a rugby league club. Parsons was never selected again and joined St Helens RL later the same year.
- **Ben Edwards** didn't take long to make his mark in international rugby. A minute into his debut against Ireland at the Arms Park on 10th March 1951, the big Newport lock kicked a long range penalty to give Wales the lead.

  Edwards had two more penalty attempts, but failed to hit the mark. He wasn't capped again.
- **Denzil Thomas** had every reason to be miffed about not playing for Wales again following his match-winning debut against Ireland in Dublin on 13th March 1954. With the scores tied at 9–9, the Llanelli centre dropped a last minute goal to clinch a 12–9 success. He was one of six new caps at Lansdowne Road – and the only one never to play again.
- **Wynne Evans** made it a double debut for the Llanelli half-backs when he joined Carwyn James against the Australians in Cardiff on 4th January 1958. Evans didn't get another call as Cardiff's Lloyd Williams resumed his club partnership with Cliff Morgan.
- **David Weaver** won the first of his two Test caps for Wales against England at Twickenham in 1964. That game ended in a 9–9 draw and the Swansea wing did play once more for Wales in an uncapped victory over Fiji later that year. But he had to wait eight years, when he was 30, before winning his second Test cap – for Zambia against Argentina in 1972.
- **Bobby Wanbon** made a telling impact on his Wales debut when

he crashed over for a try in an 11–11 draw against England at Twickenham on 20th January 1968. The Aberavon No 8 then joined St Helen's RL almost immediately after winning his Union cap.

- **David Bishop** had the distinction of scoring the only Test try against the 1984 Grand Slam Wallabies on his Wales debut at the Arms Park on 24th November. The Pontypool scrum half was deputising for arch-rival Terry Holmes, who was recovering from a dislocated shoulder.
- **Richard Rees** scored two of the eight tries on his Wales debut against Zimbabwe in Harare on 6th June 1998. Wales won 49–11, but the Swansea wing didn't get another chance.

— THE PONTYPOOL FRONT ROW —

The first time an entire Wales front row was selected from one club came on 18th January 1975 when Pontypool's Charlie Faulkner, Bobby Windsor and Graham Price all turned out against France at Parc des Princes.

The two props, Faulkner and Price, were making their Test debuts as they guided Wales to a famous 25–10 victory. Altogether the Pontypool front-row unit were selected en bloc for 19 of Wales' next 23 internationals over the following four years. Together they won 14 games and lost just five.

Since their last appearance together in 1979, only five Welsh teams have featured complete front rows from one club.

One Club Welsh front rows:

3rd June 1987 Wales 40, Canada 9 Invercargill
Cardiff: Jeff Whitefoot, Alan Phillips, Steve Blackmore

3 March 1990 Wales 9, Scotland 13 Cardiff
Neath: Brian Williams, Kevin Phillips, Jeremy Pugh

18th Nov 2000 Wales 42, USA 11 Cardiff
Swansea: Darren Morris, Garin Jenkins, Ben Evans

19th June 2004 Argentina 20, Wales 35 Buenos Aires
Ospreys: Duncan Jones, Huw Bennett, Adam Jones

17th June 2006 Argentina 45, Wales 27 Buenos Aires
Ospreys: Duncan Jones, Huw Bennett, Adam Jones

— THE BANCROFTS —

If England, Scotland and Ireland had thought they had seen the last of the Bancrofts when Billy retired (see *Men of the Decades, the 1890s: Billy Bancroft*, page 28), they were wrong. Hot on his heels came younger brother Jack, who helped himself to more glory.

Following in the great family tradition, Jack played full back for Wales in 18 Tests. While his brother had won his first cap at 19, Jack had to wait until he was 30 to get his chance.

When it came, it came in exactly the same circumstances as his brother. Billy came into the Welsh team against Scotland in 1890 as a replacement for the injured Tom England. Nineteen years on, Jack was drafted into the side when Bert Winfield withdrew with a dislocated thumb. He was an instant success and scored a Welsh record 22 points in his first Championship season as Wales became the first country to complete back-to-back Triple Crowns.

In fact, it was a second successive Grand Slam for the Welsh as they beat France as well. The following year's encounter against the French in 1910 was the first 'official' Championship match between the two countries and Bancroft kicked a record eight conversions and helped himself to a record 19 points – a haul not matched until Keith Jarrett equalled it on his debut against England in 1967.

There was another Grand Slam and Triple Crown to celebrate in 1911, with Bancroft contributing 13 points in three games. Jack also went on to match his brother's achievement of captaining Wales in 1912.

His final Test came against France in 1914 at the ripe old age of 35 and his five conversions in a 31–0 victory took his world points record to 88. That tally stood as a Welsh record for 60 years until Barry John beat it.

Between them the Bancroft brothers made 51 appearances for Wales, scored 148 points, held the world points record for 29 years and the Welsh points record for 81 years. With four Triple Crowns and two Grand Slams between them, they qualify as the most successful band of brothers to ever play for Wales.

— MEN OF THE DECADES, THE 1980s: ROB NORSTER —

In the world of the line-out jungle, in the 1980s one man bestrode it like a colossus – Rob Norster. Twice a British Lion, he equalled Allan Martin's record of 34 caps for a Wales lock and was voted both the UK and Welsh Player of the Year in 1988. It was no coincidence that Wales won the Triple Crown that season, missing out on a Grand Slam by a point to the French, and the Cardiff second row was the springboard for much of that success.

His ball-winning ability in the middle of the line meant only the likes of Maurice Colclough and Gary Whetton could rival him around the world. But as well as a high level of skill, there was also a hard edge to his game. Not that you would have believed that from a quote he gave when he later became manager of the Welsh team. "Don't ask me about emotions in the Welsh dressing room. I'm someone who cries when he watches *Little House on the Prairie,*" he said in 1994.

His playing career began in his home town team of Abertillery. He was treading in well worn family shoes at the time as four uncles played for the club and Harold Norster played in the combined Abertillery and Cross Keys team that met New Zealand in 1935.

Norster moved on to Cardiff from Abertillery in 1978 and made his first appearance against the All Blacks for his new club in that year. He toured the United States and Canada with the Welsh squad in 1980, but had a disastrous start to his Test career when he was on the losing side to the Scots in Cardiff in 1982.

But things got better. There were six wins and a draw in seven outings against England, including a key performance in the last Welsh win at Twickenham in 1988, third place in the inaugural Rugby World Cup in 1987 and that Triple Crown and shared championship in 1988. In all, he played 34 times for Wales, more than any other player in the eighties, and notched 20 wins. He was vice-captain and pack leader in 1988 and skippered the tour party to New Zealand later that year where he became Wales' 99th Test captain.

He had been to New Zealand with the Lions in 1983, where he played in the first two Tests. He was also a Lion in Australia in 1989, but only figured in the first Test.

He would have beaten Martin's lock record had it not been for an unfortunate sending-off for Cardiff against South Wales Police in 1985. The draconian WRU disciplinary standards at the time meant any player sent-off could not be considered for international duty and he missed the 1985 Five Nations championship.

At club level, he played 253 times for Cardiff and captained them for two seasons. He played in the 1982, 1984, 1986 and 1987 WRU Challenge Cup winning sides and also helped the Blues and Blacks win the unofficial Welsh club championship in 1982.

He went on to become the Wales team manager in 1991 and, in tandem with coach Alan Davies, steered his side to the 1994 Five Nations title. He resigned that post prior to the 1995 Rugby World Cup, became Cardiff team manager in 1999 and is currently chief executive of Cardiff Blues.

— DECADE BY DECADE: THE 1980s —

Played 60 Won 30 Drew 1 Lost 29
Tries: 87–80
Win percentage: 50%
Triple Crown in 1988
Third in 1987 Rugby World Cup
Beat Australia in 1981 (18–13) and 1987 (22–21)
Most appearances: Rob Norster (Cardiff) 34
Most tries: Adrian Hadley (Cardiff) 9
Most points: Paul Thorburn (Neath) 208
Most games as captain: David Pickering (Llanelli) 8
Most individual wins: Rob Norster (Cardiff) 20

— NOT YOU AGAIN! —

The 1947/48 Wallabies must have been sick of the sight of Bill Tamplin, Jack Matthews and Bleddyn Williams. The three Cardiff players met the tourists three times at Cardiff Arms Park and won on each occasion.

They were in Cardiff side that beat the Aussies 11–3, lock forward Tamplin kicked the two penalties that earned Wales a 6–0 victory in a game in which Matthews and Williams teamed-up again at centre and all three were in the Barbarians side that won the inaugural end of tour clash with the departing Test team.

— 50-POINT PASTINGS —

Wales first conceded 50 points in a match when they were beaten 52–3 by New Zealand in the first Test in Christchurch in 1988. On a miserable day for Welsh rugby they also leaked a then record ten tries, four of them to John Kirwan.

Two weeks later the All Blacks ran up 54 points in the second Test in Auckland, Wales restricting them to a mere eight tries on this occasion.

Then the Wallabies got in on the act, whalloping Wales 63–6 in Brisbane in 1991 with 12 tries – and all that before the try was upgraded to five points!

But the lowest point in Welsh rugby history came in Pretoria in 1998 when the world champion Springboks ran riot and scored 15 tries in a 96–13 victory.

Here's the complete record of Wales' 50-point nightmares, up to and including the August 2007 World Cup warm-up disaster at the hands of England:

Year	Score	Tries conceded	Opposition	Venue
1988	52–3	10	New Zealand	Lancaster Park, Christchurch
1988	54–9	8	New Zealand	Eden Park, Auckland
1991	63–6	12	Australia	Ballymore, Brisbane
1996	56–25	7	Australia	Ballymore, Brisbane
1998	96–13	15	South Africa	Pretoria
1998	60–26	8	England	Twickenham
1998	51–0	7	France	Wembley
2002	50–10	5	England	Twickenham
2002	54–10	6	Ireland	Lansdowne Road, Dublin
2003	55–3	8	New Zealand	Hamilton
2003	53–37	8	New Zealand	Sydney (World Cup)
2004	53–18	7	South Africa	Pretoria
2007	62–5	9	England	Twickenham

— THE BIG FIVE —

After a particularly poor championship campaign in 1924 there was a public outcry in Wales. The team had equalled its worst losing sequence with four championship defeats in a row – the last game in 1923 and the first three in 1924 – and the only salvation was victory over France in Paris.

Something had to be done and the WRU set up a special sub-committee at the end of the championship to 'consider whether the present method of selecting international players can be improved'. At the union's AGM in June the sub-committee's recommendation for creating a panel of five selectors was accepted – the 'Big Five' was born. The system lasted until the nineties.

The first panel was chosen on 1st September 1924, and consisted of Tommy Schofield (Bridgend), James Jarrett (Cwmbran), Ifor Thomas (Cardiff), RP Thomas (Llanelli) and DB Jones (Swansea). The first game they had to select for was against New Zealand, which ended in a 19–0 hammering. The 1925 championship campaign wasn't much better, either, as Wales lost to England, Scotland and Ireland once again.

The 'Big Five', however, grew in stature and became a much revered institution.

— BULLER STADDEN —

'Buller' Stadden has the distinction of scoring Wales' first ever drop goal against Ireland in 1884. Stadden scored the historic kick whilst making the first of his eight appearances for Wales, marking his final game by scoring the try that earned Wales their first victory over England in 1890.

Cardiff-born, Stadden launched his career with his home town team before joining Dewsbury. The Yorkshire club were renowned for playing 'generous expenses' and Stadden played 21 times for Yorkshire while he was at the club.

The victory over England came on the Dewsbury club ground, Crown Flatt, and Stadden, playing at half-back, was accused of cheating by the English. Pretending to throw the ball long into a line-out, Stadden instead dropped it short of the first forward, regathered and raced to score. This controversial ploy was made illegal in 1906, when the act of bouncing the ball from touch was outlawed.

— CHARVIS JOINS THE WING MEN —

Colin Charvis: the highest try-scoring Welsh forward

Colin Charvis leads the way for Welsh forwards in try scoring and his 20 touchdowns rank him alongside Gerald Davies and Gareth Edwards in fourth place overall on the Welsh all-time list.

The back row man's greatest achievement came when he joined

the Wales' try scoring elite by crossing the Japanese line four times at the Millennium Stadium in 2004. That feat ranked him with Wales' great try scoring wings who had matched Willie Llewellyn's record four tries on his debut against England at Swansea in 1899.

Charvis remains the one forward to have a share of the individual try scoring record, and at the time of going to print was only one try short of the world record for a forward.

Wales' four try heroes:

Willie Llewellyn	v England, Swansea, 1899
Reggie Gibbs	v France, Cardiff, 1908
Maurice Richards	v England, Cardiff, 1969
Ieuan Evans	v Canada, Invercargill, RWC 1987
Nigel Walker	v Portugal, Lisbon, RWC 1995 qualifier
Gareth Thomas	v Italy, Treviso, 1999
Shane Williams	v Japan, Osaka, 2001
Tom Shanklin	v Romania, Cardiff, 2004
Colin Charvis	v Japan, Cardiff, 2004

— GOT IT TAPED —

Scotland were Triple Crown champions in 1895, but they could have lost to Wales at Raeburn Place had a try been credited to Frank Mills. The pitch had been frozen solid overnight and many of the Welsh players felt it was unplayable.

But the game was given the go-ahead by English referee E.B. Holmes after he agreed to a suggestion by the Welsh captain Arthur Gould that the pitch be shortened by 15 or 20 yards so that the particularly icy area behind the posts at one end was taken out of play.

The referee taped out new lines on the revised pitch and the game proceeded. Billy Bancroft gave away a try when he had his kick charged down and Arthur Gould slipped when he had the line at his mercy and nobody to beat. But the key moment came when Cardiff forward Mills stretched for a try at the short end. The Welsh players felt he had reached the tape, but the referee ruled that the tape had been stretched and refused to give a try.

Scotland held on and won the game 5–4.

— DAI'S AN ENGLISHMAN —

Dai Gent was born in Llandovery, but played his rugby at Gloucester. There were so many good scrum halves in Wales at the turn of the century – Llewellyn Lloyd, Dickie Owen, Tommy Vile – that he found it difficult to break into the national side.

He played in a Welsh trial for the Probables on 20th November 1905 when Dickie Owen withdrew in the build-up to the game against New Zealand in December. The Probables were beaten 18–9 by the Possibles and the selectors ordered a second trial on 2nd December.

On the day the second trial took place Gent was making his Test debut – for England against the All Blacks at Crystal Palace in a 15–0 defeat. He played against Wales, and Owen, at Richmond in 1906, but ended up on the losing side again. He picked up a third defeat against Ireland in the next international and had to wait almost four years for his next chance.

But that was his big opportunity. Owen may have been winning his 29th cap, and Wales may have been seeking to extend their record run of 11 successive victories, but England were breaking new ground at Twickenham.

Gent was recalled to partner the Harlequins star Adrian Stoop at half-back and the home side scored immediately from the kick-off. By the end of the game Gent had finally played on a winning England side and got the better of Owen. It was the first time England had beaten Wales in 12 years.

Gent got one more cap, in the drawn game against Ireland, before exiting the Test arena, as a player at least. He helped Gloucestershire win the County Championship in 1912, became a headmaster in Maidstone and a freelance reporter for *The Sunday Times* in 1919. He wrote on rugby for 36 years, travelling the world with the British Lions and covering every Five Nations tournament up to 1955.

— PUMA POUNDING ON THE PAMPAS —

Wales won in Argentina for the first time when Graham Henry's 1999 tourists staged one of the greatest comebacks on foreign soil.

After being down and, in all probability out, by conceding 23 points in the opening 35 minutes, Rob Howley's team fought back to triumph 36–26 on their way to becoming the first team from the Four Home Unions to win an away series against the Pumas as they took the second Test 23–16.

— IN-FIGHTING —

Just about the only fight Wales showed at Ballymore in 1991, when they leaked 12 tries in a then record 63–6 defeat by Australia, came at the after-match function.

Unfortunately, they only managed to fight amongst themselves in the wake of their humiliation with two future captains, Gareth Llewellyn and Mike Hall, in the thick of the action. It all happened much to the bemusement of the Wallabies who had escaped without suffering any similar damage on the field.

— WHAT A DEBUT —

When it comes to making your mark on your debut, then nobody has quite matched the great Willie Llewellyns' feat of scoring four tries against England in 1899.

But Wales' record cap holder Gareth Thomas went pretty close in his first game for Wales in the opening match of the 1995 Rugby World Cup in Bloemfontein. A mere 96 years on from Willie's great day, Thomas winged in for a hat-trick to launch his assault on the Welsh try scoring record.

While both Llewellyn and Thomas had the full match to harvest their tries, Byron Hayward came on as a third minute replacement in the 1998 tour match against Zimbabwe in Harare and finished with a hat-trick.

And, when Tony Clement made his Wales debut as a 66th minute replacement in the 1987 match against the USA Eagles, he found his brief 14 minutes on the pitch profitable enough to score two tries on debut. Clement scored two of the eight Welsh tries to join Dickie Ralph in the record books, Ralph having crossed twice in his first outing in the 1931 win over France at St Helen's.

— FEVER PITCH —

London Welsh forward Jack Williams was one of the heroes who helped to beat New Zealand in 1905. He won four caps and also faced the Springboks in 1906.

He won a Test cap on the Anglo-Welsh 'Lions' tour to Australia and New Zealand in 1908 and captained his club in the 1907/08 season; but he met an untimely death in Nigeria while working for the Colonial Service. He contracted blackwater fever and died in 1911 at the age of 28.

— DAI 'TARW' JONES —

If a win over New Zealand is the most priceless possession any Welsh rugby player can take to his grave, then Dai 'Tarw' Jones is unique. For not only did he play his part in Wales' immortal 3–0 win over the first All Blacks in 1905, he also scored a try in the Wales XIII victory over the pioneering 'All Golds' in 1908.

Jones was one of the biggest men to play for Wales in his era, an iron-hard collier-turned policeman-turned licensee who stood 6ft 1in tall and weighed in at 15st 4lbs. He made his Wales debut at the age of 20 against England in the first Welsh victory at Blackheath and was never on the losing side against the men in white. He won three Triple Crowns, starred in the only team to beat Dave Gallaher's 1905 All Black tourists and lost in only tow of his 13 internationals.

But that's only half the story. Capped initially from Treherbert, he won his last four caps from Aberdare and came under suspicion for taking illegal payments. A collier in Aberaman, he quit Treherbert to captain Aberdare for two seasons from 1905 at 10 shillings a week plus train fares and meals. When mounting debts forced the Aberdare committee to cut the wages to five shillings a week, Jones promptly moved back to Treherbert.

The WRU launched a full-scale inquiry into alleged 'professionalism' in the valley clubs and, while their report found those allegations 'not proven', it did lead to the suspension of the entire committees of Aberdare and Treorchy, who had been charged with match fixing.

Six players were temporarily suspended, but Jones was the biggest casualty among eight players who were permanently suspended. He was still only 26. But there was an easy solution. He didn't have to move, he simply joined the Treherbert Northern Union club.

He then switched to Merthyr Tydfil and found himself lining-up against New Zealand again in the first rugby league international match between two countries.

When the 'All Golds' lined up at Aberdare on New Year's Day, 1908, it was the first time a touring team had played a rugby league international. Jones was one of four Welsh-based players in the Welsh XIII and he scored the winning try to help Wales win 9–8 in front of 17,000 fans.

That performance earned him a place in the first Great Britain rugby league side that met the New Zealanders at Leeds on 25th January,1908. It brought Jones another win over his great adversaries, 14–6, before he signed off with a first international defeat against

New Zealand in the Second Test, 6–18 at Chelsea. He followed that with a 35–18 triumph over England at Tonypandy on 20th April – his fourth international success over the English – before bringing his international career in the two codes to an end with 17 caps, 14 wins and 3 defeats.

Jones served with the Welsh Guards in the First World War and was seriously injured at the Battle off the Somme. He remains the only man to play for Wales in victories over New Zealand in both codes.

— SPEEDY IEUAN —

You had to be quick to keep up with Llanelli wing Ieuan Evans and most defences found him too hot to handle. He holds the record for scoring the two quickest tries in Welsh rugby history. He crossed the Irish line after a mere 33 seconds in 1997 and the Japanese line in 46 seconds in 1993.

However, not even Evans could hold back Scottish centre John Leslie when he helped himself to the quickest Five/Six Nations try of all time at Murrayfield when Wales were the visitors in 1999. Leslie crossed for the first of the game's six tries in 9.5 seconds – half a second faster than Leo Price's freak try for England against Wales at Twickenham in 1923.

Another opposition player to be quick off the mark was Canada's Bobby Ross who hit Wales with a quickfire drop goal after only 16 seconds on 19th July 1997.

Quick tries for Wales:

Date	**Time**	**Player**	**Opposition**
1st Feb 1997	33 secs	Ieuan Evans	Ireland
16th Oct 1993	46 secs	Ieuan Evans	Japan

Quick tries against Wales:

Date	**Time**	**Player**	**Country**
6th Feb 1999	9.5 secs	John Leslie	Scotland
20th Jan 1923	10 secs	Leo Price	England
9th June 1996	54 secs	Joe Roff	Australia

— IT'S A RECORD —

On 18th March 1899, a world record rugby crowd of 40,000 packed into the Arms Park in Cardiff to see Wales play Ireland. The Irish were chasing the Triple Crown and the crowd scenes before and during the game were remarkable.

The pitch had to be cleared of fans before the game could kick-off and half-time lasted 15 minutes as stewards pushed fans back off the touchlines.

The game was held up a number of times in the second half because the fans were creeping onto the pitch. The Irish won 3–0 to take the Triple Crown for the second time.

— RONNIE A BIG HIT AT THE ARMS PARK —

Big time boxing first came to Cardiff Arms Park on 12th August 1944, when Swansea's Ronnie James took the British Lightweight title away from Eric Boon. James won in the 10th round when the referee stopped the fight.

It would be 49 years before boxing, in the ring at least, returned to the ground, when Lennox Lewis beat Frank Bruno in a world heavyweight bout in 1993. Amir Khan and Joe Calzaghe have both fought at the Millennium Stadium.

— THE IRISH TROUBLES —

Every member of the Welsh party that went to Dublin to conclude the 1923 Five Nations championship had to be insured for £1,000 because of the political troubles in Ireland at the time.

Several members of the WRU General Committee were stopped and searched by the military in Sackville Street on the Friday night before the game. The only 'concealed weapon' found among them was a toothpick. However, the team were told that rebel snipers were operating from the roof of a building near their hotel. The Irish won 5–4 to condemn Wales to their worst season since 1892 and the dreaded wooden spoon.

In 1972, because of increased violence in Ulster and the possible repercussions in the south, Wales and Scotland decided not to risk travelling to Dublin. Wales won the title that season with wins over England, Scotland and France, but missed out on a possible Grand Slam as a result of the cancellation of the scheduled game at Lansdowne Road.

— MEN OF THE DECADES, THE 1990s: NEIL JENKINS —

Neil Jenkins notches some of his world record 1,049 international points

When Neil Jenkins finally bowed out of international rugby on 1st November 2002 he had scored a world record 1,049 points for his country in 87 Tests. He had obliterated Australian Michael Lynagh's mark of 911 points along the way and averaged 12 points per international with his 41 in four Test appearances for the British and Irish Lions taking him to 1,090 points in 91 major internationals.

He left with a formidable legacy of 'mosts' for his country: most points (1,049), most conversions (130), most penalty goals (231), most points in a match (30), most penalty goals in a match (9) and most dropped goals in a match (3).

The 'Ginger Monster', as he became known, scored 5,557 points in his senior club and international career spanning 431 matches. He played for Wales Youth, Wales Under-21 and made his senior Wales debut against England at Cardiff Arms Park on 19th January 1991.

He was one of two teenagers in the Welsh back division on that day, joining his former Wales Youth team-mate Scott Gibbs. If it was an inauspicious start for the pair – England won 25–6 to end a 28-year run in Cardiff without a win - they certainly hit the high spots later in their careers.

Gibbs won 53 caps in a career that also saw him join St Helens for three years, but returned to join Jenkins in the 1997 British and Irish Lions Test series-winning squad in South Africa.

Then they teamed up at Wembley to help Wales famously deny England a Grand Slam in 1999. Gibbs waltzed over for the try (see *Woody's Wembley Woes*, page 25) and then handed the ball to Jenkins to kick the winning goal. If that was Gibbs' most famous try, picking the most famous of Jenkins' kicks is probably impossible. His kicking from full back for the Lions in South Africa effectively won the series and he had the honour of scoring the first points at the Millennium Stadium when he landed the first penalty.

He steered his home town team of Pontypridd to Welsh Cup and League honours, took them to a European Challenge Cup final and also starred for Cardiff and the Celtic Warriors.

When he pulled on a Welsh jersey for the final time as a 64th minute replacement in the uncapped game against the Barbarians at the Millennium Stadium on 31st May 2003, he had made exactly 100 appearances for his country – 87 Tests, ten tour matches and three matches for a Wales XV. Yet, while he was the mainstay of the Welsh team for more than a decade, he suffered setbacks along the way. He was left out of the 1991 Rugby World Cup teams as Mark Ring filled the No 10 jersey and he played centre and full back for his country as Adrian Davies and Arwel Thomas got runs at outside half.

But when Graham Henry took over as coach he had one man in mind to play in the pivotal role. He made Jenkins play closer to the gain line and he played the best rugby of his career. Wales won ten games in a row, won in France for the first time in 24 years and beat England at Wembley. Jenkins broke Lynagh's world record at the

Millennium Stadium on 14th October 1999 in the Rugby World Cup defeat by Samoa and also joined Henry in Australia on the 2000 Lions tour.

Whenever the debate about the ultimate Welsh outside half rages, Jenkins' impressive credentials mean he always figures in the argument.

— WALES' RECORD IN THE 1990s —

Played 98 Won 48 Drew 1 Lost 49
Tries: 230–259
Win percentage: 48.98%
Outright Championship win in 1994
Beat South Africa in 1999 (29–19)
Most appearances: Neil Jenkins (Pontypridd/Cardiff) 73
Most tries: Ieuan Evans (Llanelli) 26
Most points: Neil Jenkins (Pontypridd/Cardiff) 895
Most games as captain: Ieuan Evans (Llanelli) 28
Most individual wins: Neil Jenkins (Pontypridd/Cardiff) 37

— POACHERS TURNED GAMEKEEPERS —

Nine Welsh international players have gone on to be international referees in the union code. One other became a Test referee in rugby league.

English-born John Griffin won his only Welsh cap in Scotland when he was called up at the last minute from Edinburgh University to fill a space in the Welsh side in 1883. He later emigrated to South Africa where he took charge of the first Test played in that country.

Name	Caps as a player	As international referee
Charles Lewis	5 caps, 1882–84	1 Test, 1885
Horace Lyne	5 caps, 1883–85	1 Test, 1885
William Phillips	5 caps, 1881–84	2 Tests, 1887–89
Billy Douglas	4 caps, 1886–87	4 Tests, 1891–1903
John Griffin	1 cap, 1883	1 Test, 1891
Tom Williams	1 cap, 1882	1 Test, 1904
Harry Bowen	4 caps, 1882–87	1 Test, 1905
Gwyn Nicholls	24 caps, 1896–1906	1 Test, 1909
Tommy Vile	8 caps, 1908–21	12 Tests, 1923–31

* Billy McCutcheon refereed rugby league Tests in 1908–09.

— KEEP THE COAL FIRES BURNING —

England nearly didn't bother travelling to Cardiff for their championship opener in January 1893. The weather was so bad that the Cardiff Arms Park pitch was frozen solid and it seemed impossible that the game could be played.

The Welsh Rugby Union secretary Bill Gwynn sought a solution and found one in conjunction with the Arms Park groundsman. After experimenting with a small fire on the heavily protected ground, it was found the pitch could be softened.

Gwynn sent a telegram to the RFU saying there was a chance that the game could be played and the England party left Paddington Station at 5.45pm on Friday afternoon. When they arrived in Cardiff, accompanied by a blizzard, they could hardly believe what they saw at the ground. There were 500 'fire devils' blazing furiously over the pitch, with 40 boiler plates helping to spread the heat. Eighteeen tons of coal were burned overnight to soften the surface.

This is how a local newspaper painted the picture of the scene to its readers:

> *"From an early hour on Friday morning a large number of men – mostly drawn from the unemployed class – were engaged to lay down and trim more than 500 devils (braziers), extemporised out of buckets pierced with holes and fixed on bricks. Although there was slight snow during the night, the intense heat from the devils softened the ground in a manner far exceeding the most sanguine expectations. When darkness set in, the spectacle was an exceedingly picturesque one and the field was visited by a large number of football enthusiasts."*
>
> *Saturday morning was cold again and the groundsman and his team of helpers had to remove the braziers and take the straw covering off the field. They worked until 11am. The blackened turf was soft enough to convince the referee, the ex-Scottish captain and then President, Douglas Morton that the game could go ahead. A crowd of 17,000 people braved the elements and were rewarded with a fantastic match."*

In the 1980s, the WRU installed undersoil heating at the Arms Park to prevent losing matches to freezing conditions. Twenty miles of copper piping were laid nine inches below the surface to avoid a big freeze like the one in 1893.

— A FAIR WIND FOR WALES —

In 1874 a ship bound for the United States foundered in the Irish Sea and took safe haven in Milford Haven. On board was the O'Neill family from Cork.

Not wishing to push their luck they decided to remain in Wales and worked their way to Cardiff.

Four years later they had a son, Billy, who went on to become an Arms Park legend. 'Billy Neill', as he was always known, played for 11 seasons at Cardiff, scoring 17 tries in 204 appearances, helping them to beat South Africa 21–0 in 1906 and becoming the first forward to make more than 200 appearances for the club.

He won 11 caps in the second row for Wales, winning ten games and losing only once in 1904 – to Ireland! He helped Wales win the Triple Crown in 1905 and become the first country to complete the Grand Slam in 1908.

After that, at the age of 30, he joined Warrington rugby league club. He made his club debut on 17th October 1908, and then won the first of his two Welsh rugby league caps against England at Broughton Park 71 days later.

— QUICK CHANGE —

Newport forward Horace Lyne won the last of his five caps against England at St Helen's on 3rd January 1885. Less than a month later he met up once again with the majority of the English team – as referee of their next match.

Lyne became a legend of rugby administration after his playing days, which included captaining Newport and winning the South Wales Challenge Cup. He served on the WRU General Committee from 1885 and was Chairman of Newport Athletic Club for 55 years.

A founder member of the International Rugby Board, he was a board member from 1887 to 1938, making him the longest serving member in conjunction with Ireland's Robert Warren – a man he had played against in the 1884 clash between Wales and Ireland in Cardiff.

Lyne was President of the WRU from 1906 to 1947 and he was presented with the Freedom of the Borough of Newport in 1934 on his retirement after 50 years of service as the Chief Fire Officer of Newport.

— MEN OF THE DECADES, THE 2000s: GARETH THOMAS —

If Ieuan Evans was the talisman for the Welsh team in the 1990s, then Gareth Thomas took over his mantle as rugby moved into the 21st century. Not only that, but Thomas eclipsed Evans' Welsh try-scoring record and in 2005 spurred his side on to a first Grand Slam in 27 years.

The former Bridgend postman developed into a world class player and a top class leader. A product of the same Pencoed Youth team that spawned Scott Gibbs, Gareth Cooper and Gavin Henson, he won two caps for Wales Youth in 1993 before making his senior debut with Bridgend.

It didn't take him long to make his mark on the senior game, winning caps at Under 21 level before graduating into the full Wales side for the 1995 Rugby World Cup in South Africa. His Test debut came against Japan in Bloemfontein and he notched a hat-trick playing on the wing.

His ability to play in different positions has been one of the keys to his longevity and up to the game against Argentina in August 2007 he had made 57 appearances on the wing (three as sub), 19 at full back (one as sub) and 20 at centre (one as sub).

Thomas broke Evans' try scoring record with his 33rd score at Twickenham in 2004 and marked his record breaking 93rd appearance, overtaking Gareth Llewellyn, with his 38th try in the first Test in Australia in 2007.

With three Test caps for the British and Irish Lions in New Zealand in 2005, including one try, he is poised to become the first Welsh player to play in 100 internationals – and only the fourth northern hemisphere player after Jason Leonard, Fabien Pelous and Philippe Sella.

Thomas turned into a full back by accident after being dropped for the Rugby World Cup game against New Zealand in Sydney in 2003. Shane Williams and Tom Shanklin won the wing spots and Garan Evans was given the full back berth. But when Evans was badly injured after only four minutes, Thomas came on at the back and played a blinder. That was the start of a run of 14 appearances in the No 15 jersey.

It was Steve Hansen who first handed him the captain's armband, for the Rugby World Cup warm-up game in Ireland, although it would be another 14 months before he led his country again. From the joker in the squad, Thomas turned into the model professional and his dedication and determination were brought to the fore by Hansen. His move to Toulouse earned him a Heineken Cup winner's medal in

2005 and his reputation grew markedly during his three seasons on the continent.

His near length of the field interception try against Australia in 1996 ranks as the longest run in by any Welsh player and he also bagged a try on the opening day at the Millennium Stadium in 1999. He also scored a record equalling four tries against Italy in Treviso.

'Alfie', as he is affectionately known throughout the rugby playing world, took over the captaincy of the Lions for the final two Tests in 2005 when Brian O'Driscoll was injured and was Welsh Player of the Year in 2003 and 2004.

— WALES' RECORD IN THE 2000s —

Played 89 Won 39 Drew 3 Lost 47
Tries: 275–271
Win percentage: 43.82%
Grand Slam/Triple Crown in 2005
Outright championship win in 2005
Beat Australia in 2005 (24–22)
Most appearances: Colin Charvis (Dragons) 60
Most tries: Shane Williams (Ospreys) 29
Most points: Stephen Jones (Scarlets) 538
Most games as captain: Colin Charvis (Dragons) 22
Most individual wins: Colin Charvis (Dragons), Gareth Thomas (Toulouse) 25

— THANKS FOR THE MEMORIES —

The 174th and final Welsh international at the National Ground, Cardiff Arms Park, was against England on 15th March 1997. A month later, after Cardiff had beaten Swansea in the final of the WRU Challenge Cup in the last game staged on the old ground, the bulldozers moved in and the way was cleared for the Millennium Stadium.

It was a day when the game said fond farewells to more than just the Arms Park. England legends Will Carling and Rob Andrew played their final games in white and Welsh superstar Jonathan Davies ended his second stint as a union international.

England won at a canter, 34–13, but Rob Howley at least salvaged some Welsh pride by scoring the final international try at the Arms Park – 113 years on from the first scored by another Cardiff player, wing William Norton.

— BRING ON THE SUBS —

Phil Bennett: the first ever Welsh replacement

Phil Bennett became the first replacement used by Wales when he came onto the field at Stade Colombes on 22nd March,1969, to win his first cap with four minutes remaining when centre Gerald Davies dislocated his elbow.

The number of replacements available to a team has grown to seven and now it is not uncommon for coaches to use a complete bench in a match. Gethin Jenkins holds the record for the number of appearances as a replacement with 21 in a Test career of 47 caps up to August 18th 2007.

Andrew Williams holds the record for the most caps as a replacement without making a Test start. He won his fifth cap as a substitute in Brisbane in the second test of the 2007 summer tour, overtaking David Llewellyn and Gareth Delve.

Name	Career	Reps	Starts	Caps
Ceri Sweeney	2003–2007	20	11	31
Dwayne Peel	2001–2007	19	34	53
Gethin Jenkins	2002–2007	19	26	45
Mefin Davies	2002–2006	18	21	39
Jonathan Thomas	2003–2007	17	17	34
Andrew Lewis	1996–2002	16	13	29
Barry Williams	1996–2002	15	9	24
Chris Wyatt	1998–2003	13	25	38
Spencer John	1995–2002	12	6	18
Mike Phillips	2003–2007	12	10	22
Duncan Jones	2001–2007	12	26	38

— DRUGS SHAME —

Former Wales 'B' and South Wales Police centre Richie Griffiths picked up an unenviable first for himself and Welsh rugby in December 1991, when he became the first player in world rugby to test positive for an anabolic steroid. The 27-year-old was banned for two years when traces of nandrolone were found in his sample given after he had scored a try in his side's 17–13 win over Aberavon in a league game. He returned two years later to play for Maesteg.

— OVER TO YOU, GODSON —

Mervyn Davies had a special reason to feel proud when Scott Quinnell surpassed his record of 38 caps as Wales' most capped No 8 against Ireland in Dublin in 2002.

Because while it was well known that Scott had a famous father (Derek Quinnell won 23 caps for Wales and went on three Lions tours) and uncle (Barry John won 25 Welsh caps and was a Lion on two tours), it wasn't widely known that Mervyn Davies was the young Quinnell's godfather.

— THE BEST OF TIMES: 10 OUT OF 10 —

Wales enjoyed a run of ten straight wins under coach Graham Henry between 6th March and 9th October 1999. The winning streak began with Wales' first win on French soil for 24 years and included five away wins at the start.

As well as winning in Paris, Henry's team triumphed in Italy, Argentina (twice) and Wembley.

Henry's top ten:
France 33 Wales 34, Paris
Italy 21 Wales 60, Treviso
Wales 32 England 31, Wembley
Argentina 26 Wales 36, Buenos Aires
Argentina 16 Wales 23, Buenos Aires
Wales 29 South Africa 19, Cardiff
Wales 33 Canada 19, Cardiff
Wales 34 France 23, Cardiff
Wales 23 Argentina 18, Cardiff (RWC)
Wales 64 Japan 15, Cardiff (RWC)

Sadly, the great run ended in a bit of a whimper as Wales were beaten 38–31 by Samoa in their third and final Pool D match in the World Cup.

— THE WORST OF TIMES: 0 OUT OF 10 —

Wales suffered the worst run of defeats in their history when they lost ten games on the trot under coach Steve Hansen between 23rd November 2002 and 23rd August 2003 – the run starting and ending with home defeats.

Also included in the sequence was Wales' 48–35 defeat by the Barbarians in an uncapped match in Cardiff.

Hansen's howlers:
Wales 17 New Zealand 43, Cardiff
Italy 30 Wales 22, Rome
Wales 9 England 26, Cardiff
Scotland 30 Wales 22, Edinburgh
Wales 24 Ireland 25, Cardiff
France 33 Wales 5, Paris
Australia 30 Wales 10, Sydney
New Zealand 55 Wales 3, Hamilton
Ireland 35 Wales 12, Dublin
Wales 9 England 43, Cardiff

— POSH SCOTS —

When Scotland came to St Helen's, Swansea on 7th February 1925, they not only brought a team brim-full with talent, but also boasting a few toffs.

The Grand Slam side in the making had a future Lord in their forwards, John Bannerman, and a knight acting as touch judge, Sir Robert Mackenzie.

Wales were led by a miner, Steve Morris of Cross Keys.

— POST-MATCH MAYHEM —

There have been many notable post-match dinners following international matches across the rugby playing world, but rarely can there have been as much merry mayhem as followed the 1890 match between Ireland and Wales in Dublin.

The game was played on St David's Day and Wales were looking to avoid a third successive defeat by the Irish. With the home side leading 3–0 with only five minutes to play it looked as though it was going to be Ireland's day again. But then the Newport outside half Charlie Thomas broke clear for a try which Billy Bancroft converted to secure a 3–3 draw.

In the wake of the post-match celebrations no fewer than nine players were arrested for "too much exuberance of spirits". Eight of the players were Irish and a number of them received small fines at a Dublin court on Monday morning. The name of the sole Welsh player involved was never divulged.

— FOOT AND MOUTH —

The 2001 Six Nations Championship lasted a staggering 259 days from start to finish – Ireland postponing their three away matches on the mainland following the UK outbreak of foot and mouth.

What began on 3rd February 2001 finally ended on 20th October as Ireland made every effort to stop the disease spreading across the Irish Sea with Irish fans returning home from the Tests. The game against Wales at the Millennium Stadium was due to be played on 3rd March, but was finally played on 13th October. Ireland won 36–6.

— REFEREEING DRAMA —

Wales were chasing the Grand Slam in 1965 and had to head to Paris to beat the French to secure the prize. Irish referee Ron Gilliland was in charge of the match and had Bernard Marie (France) and Ron Lewis (Wales) running the touch lines.

No French referee had been appointed to officiate in a Five Nations game up to this point, but Marie was to change all of that. When Gilliland burst a blood vessel in his left calf after 32 minutes, with Wales trailing 13–0, one of the two touch-judges had to take over. The question was, which one?

Welsh skipper Clive Rowlands felt it would be too inflammatory to the home crowd to give Lewis the whistle and suggested the fairest way to decide would be to toss a coin.

It took the captains, officials and eventually the Presidents of the French and Welsh Unions almost ten minutes to try to decide what should happen. In the end, the chairman of the Welsh selectors, Alun Thomas, won the day by suggesting that as the French had nominated the referee in the first place they should choose his replacement.

Marie took over and made his own piece of history. Wales lost 21–13 and, in 1966, Marie was given charge of the game at Twickenham between England and Ireland to launch a long line of highly successful and respected French referees.

— UNLUCKY 13 —

The only occasion that Wales have been forced to play with 13 men due to yellow or red cards was for just two minutes against Argentina at Puerto Madrin on 11th June 2006. First, Gavin Thomas was dispatched to the sin-bin by Irish referee Alain Rolland in the 31st minute. Then his back row colleague Alix Popham was sent to the cooler eight minutes later. Argentina won the game 27–25.

— FOUR CAPTAINS —

When Wales were due to embark on a summer tour to Australia and New Zealand ahead of the 2003 Rugby World Cup, coach Steve Hansen decided to name four captains in his 30-man squad.

Colin Charvis, Martyn Williams, Robin McBryde and Stephen Jones were given the roles in a move that mirrored that used by women's hockey in Australia.

— THE IRON MAN —

Dr Jack Matthews was one of the most feared tacklers in the game, but he was also exceptionally quick. The Welsh junior 220 yards champion in 1937, he also ran in the senior championships.

'Dr Jack', as he is known around the rugby playing world, enhanced his hard man reputation during the Second World War when, as a member of the Royal Army Medical Corps, he got into the ring with an American soldier at a training camp. He successfully completed three rounds of sparring – which is more than many heavyweights managed after the war – with none other than Rocky Marciano.

On the field, 'Dr Jack' scored 54 tries in 180 games for Cardiff between 1945 and 1954, played in five Victory Internationals before winning 17 caps, won a Grand Slam in 1950 and was an ever-present in the British Lions' six Tests in New Zealand and Australia in 1950.

He scored two of his four international tries against England at St Helen's in a 23–5 win on 20th January 1951, and ran straight through the English midfield for one of the tries. As Lewis Jones stepped up to take the conversion, the Welsh touch judge overheard the English centres consoling each other. "Of course you can't stop him, he's made of iron," the one said to the other.

— WHAT'S THE SCORE? —

Having succeeded in getting Wales' weather-affected match with England to go ahead in January 1893 (see *Keep the Coal Fires Burning*, page 117), the next problem was the scoring. A try was worth three points at that time in Wales, but only two in England, Scotland and Ireland. Importantly, the International Rugby Board had met two days earlier and concluded that a try should be worth two points and all goals (penalties and conversions) should be worth three points. So two points it was.

Wales used the four three-quarter system, while England played with nine forwards. With the wind at their backs in the first half, the visitors raced ahead and scored two tries and a conversion without reply. A third try soon followed before the great Welsh revival began. Skipper Arthur Gould raced to the posts for a try which Billy Bancroft converted and then Norman Biggs added a second try.

In Welsh terms, the score was now 11–8, although it was actually 9–7 to England. A third try by Howard Marshall extended the English lead – to 14–8 in Welsh scoring and 11–7 as per thee new rules – and the first game between the two countries in Cardiff looked destined to be a win for England.

But the extra man behind the scrum began to pay dividends for Wales – so much so that English skipper Andrew Stoddart took Sam Woods out of the pack for a while to even things up behind – and a second Gould try took the score to 11–9.

As the game moved to its climax, Wales were awarded a penalty wide out on the English 25. What to do? There are reports of an argument between Gould and Bancroft on what style kick to take. Gould is alleged to have placed the ball on the ground for his full back to kick at goal, while the result was that Bancroft drop kicked the winning points. It was the first penalty goal scored by a Welsh player in the 29th international match played.

There were many in the ground who thought Bancroft's kick had secured a 14–14 draw. There was even confusion on the press bench on the touchline – until WRU Secretary Bill Gwyn went up to the journalists and explained that Welsh rules didn't apply and Wales had won!

— YOUNG GUNS IN PARIS —

The youngest Welsh team to start a Test match was the side that met France at Stade Colombes on 21st March, 1930. The average age of the side, captained by Guy Morgan, was just 22 years and 109 days. There were two teenagers in the pack, prop Edgar Jones and flanker Norman Fender. The oldest player in the side was the great Aberavon lock Ned Jenkins at 25 years, 298 days. Wales ended on a high in Paris with an 11–0 victory.

— CHECK THE SCORE —

When Wales beat England at Twickenham for the first time on 21st January 1933, the championship record crowd of 64,000 left the ground believing the score to be 9–3.

The scoreboard operator had notched the conversion by Wales full back Viv Jenkins of Ronnie Boon's second half try close to the posts. The Welsh touch judge, a member of the WRU committee, Mr Llewellyn, who was from Jenkins' home town of Bridgend, flagged the kick as over and everyone in the ground thought the kick was good.

But after the game the Irish referee, Tom Bell, said he had not allowed the goal. Wales had won 7–3.

— THORBURN'S BIG BOOT —

Paul Thorburn kicks his way into the record books

Paul Thorburn will always be remembered for his big boot, but nothing the Neath full back ever did surpassed his monster penalty against Scotland at the Arms Park on 1st February 1986.

Wales were leading 16–15 in the second half when Finlay Calder late tackled Jonathan Davies between the Welsh 22 and 10 metre line.

"I fancy my chances," Thorburn told skipper David Pickering. The wind was blowing strongly and so Pickering gave his man the chance to prove a point.

The kick carried the full distance to the posts – measured after the game at 70 yards, 8.5 inches. It remains the longest kick in the history of Welsh international rugby. Just for good measure Thorburn popped over another from three yards inside his own half to ensure Wales won 22–15.

His five penalties that day took his international points tally to 54 in only his fifth Test – one quicker than the previous Welsh record holder, Gwyn Evans, had taken to reach 50 points. Thorburn went on to re-write the Welsh points scoring records. He scored a Welsh championship record 52 points in the 1986 campaign, including a Five Nations high of 16 penalties, and was the first Welsh player to pass 200 and 300 points.

He ended with 304 Test points from 37 appearances.

— WATCH IT! —

When Newport went through the 1922/23 season unbeaten – they won 29 and drew four of their 33 games – the citizens of the town raised £500 to help mark the achievement.

Even the Prince of Wales donated a shilling to the cause and the Newport club, who donated £120, and the WRU sanctioned the action. The club decided the money should be used to present each player in skipper Jack Wetter's side with a gold watch. That was what they had done in 1892 when Tom Graham's side had remained unbeaten. The 1923 gift was valued at £21.

But the Scottish Rugby Union were not impressed and ordered Neil McPherson, their Cardiff-born international who had won the last two of his seven caps that season against Ireland and England, to return his watch.

The Scots, who had refused to play Wales in 1897 and 1898 in the wake of the Arthur Gould 'professionalism' affair, banned McPherson 'sine die' and declared that any Scottish player who played against him or any of his Newport team-mates would be professionalised.

In October 1923, the International Rugby Board decreed the WRU should not have supported the presentation and placed a ceiling figure of £2 on any future mementoes presented to players. McPherson never played for Scotland again.

— SACRÉ ROUGE! —

When Colin Charvis won his 65th cap against Scotland in Cardiff at the start of the 2004 Six Nations campaign he became the first Welsh player to be capped from a French club.

Since then Gareth Llewellyn has been capped from Narbonne, Gareth Thomas from Toulouse and Stephen Jones from ASM Clermont Auvergne. But it was Charvis who completed the full set of countries in the Five Nations from which players have been capped by Wales.

After playing for Wales against Argentina on 18th August 2007, Charvis had won 88 caps from four clubs – 59 from Swansea, five as an unattached player during the 2003 Rugby World Cup, four from Tarbes, 16 from Newcastle Falcons and four from the Dragons.

Here are the clubs from other nations who have supplied Welsh caps:

England (29): Bath, Bedford, Birkenhead Park, Blackheath, Bradford, Bristol, Cambridge University, Coventry, Devonport Services, Gloucester, Guy's Hospital, Harlequins, Harrogate, Leeds Tykes, Leicester, London Irish, Loughborough Colleges, Moseley, Northampton, Oxford University, Richmond, Sale Sharks, Somerset Police, St Barts Hospital, St Luke's College, Exeter, Torquay, Weston, Worcester

Scotland (2): Edinburgh University, Edinburgh Wanderers

Ireland (1): Bective Rangers

France (4): ASM Clermont Auvergne, Narbonne, Tarbes, Toulouse

— THE FIRST REPRESENTATIVE FIXTURE —

Castle Green, Hereford was the venue for the first representative fixture played by a Welsh team when the South Wales FC side met a Hereford XV. It was December 1875 and the Welsh team wore black and white colours.

In order to mark that game the WRU struck a special black jersey which was used as part of their 125th anniversary season celebrations, including the win over the Australians at the Millennium Stadium in November 2005.

The South Wales FC won that opening fixture by a try to nothing. The try was scored by Swansea's A.H. Richardson.

— ALL TICKET —

Interest in the Ireland v Wales match at Lansdowne Road on 8th March 1902, was so great that it became the first rugby match to be made 'all ticket'. Wales won 15–0 to claim a third Triple Crown.

The RFU made a similar move after 75,532 fans crammed into Twickenham for the championship opener between England and Wales on 21st January 1950. All future games at the stadium were all-ticket affairs. Wales won on the day, 11–5, to set up a Grand Slam campaign.

— JEREMY'S LONG WAIT —

When drug testing was introduced into rugby in the 1980s, international players were often required to provide samples immediately after matches. The Neath prop Jeremy Pugh held the record for the longest wait to give an adequate sample – four hours!

— PERCY AND THE ZULU DANCE —

When the Australians embarked on their first European tour in 1908 they were urged by the Australian Rugby Union to perform a 'war cry' before the game – something akin to the All Blacks' Haka.

The players didn't really like doing it, but their rendition before the game against Cardiff at the Arms Park on 28th December brought an amusing response from the home skipper Percy Bush.

According to Peter Sharpham, who wrote a book about that first tour, called *The First Wallabies*: "While the Australians were performing their war cry, Percy Bush responded with his own brand of mock aggression, advancing towards the tourists brandishing a Zulu spear and shield, supposedly a relic of the battle of Rorke's Drift."

The Aussies gave themselves the nickname 'Wallabies' before the first match, preferring that term to 'Waratahs' and 'Wallaroos'. They are still known as the 'Wallabies' today.

Cardiff won that game and have never been beaten by Australia.

— FOURTH CHOICE GOALKICKER —

Barry John used to kick goals for fun with his toe when he was at Gwendraeth Grammar School. But when the future Welsh points record holder, and British Lions points sensation of 1971, went into club rugby he was not considered good enough to take the kicks.

It wasn't until he toured New Zealand with the Lions that John became a regular goalkicker. In fact, the year before that historic Lions tour, John was fourth choice goalkicker at Cardiff behind Robin Williams, Denis Gethin and Gareth Edwards. And when he did get a chance to show what he could do, converting a try half-way out at Swansea, he didn't even reach the cross bar.

Having seen Wales use a hooker, Norman Gale, a flanker, John Taylor, a wing, Laurie Daniel, and part time kickers like J.P.R. Williams and Gareth Edwards, John eventually kicked a conversion for Wales in his 20th Test. Up until then he had scored 30 points, yet in his final six games he grabbed 60 more points, including13 penalties and six conversions.

His around the corner, instep style was totally different to his toe-prodding school days – "I used to wear a pair of 30 bob, Co-op boots that had a huge great flat slab across the toe when I was in school that made it hard to miss" – and his 90 points for Wales took him two past Jack Bancroft's 58 year record.

John scored a Welsh championship record 35 points in 1972 and notched a record 188 points on the 1971 Lions tour.

— THE PRESIDENT'S SON —

Glyn Stephens had been used to watching his son, Rees, playing for Wales. After all, the great Neath second row had won 28 caps between 1947-56. But the 1957 Five Nations championship was to be extra special for the Stephens family as Glyn, who had won 10 caps himself from Neath between 1912-19, was the President of the Welsh Rugby Union.

It meant that for the first time in rugby history the President of a national Union was able to watch his son play for his country's team. Wales ended with wins over Ireland and France, but lost to England and Scotland. Having lost the first two games, Wales were led in their last two matches by Stephens.

The next time a National XV had a President and player from the same family was in 1961, when Ireland's Noel Murphy was President of the IRFU and his son, Noel Arthur Murphy, was in the Irish XV.

— BIBLIOGRAPHY —

The Illustrated History of Welsh Rugby – J.G.B. Thomas (Pelham)

Rugby: Men, Matches and Moments – J.G.B. Thomas (Pelham)

Great Moments in Sport: Rugby Football – J.G.B. Thomas (Pelham)

History of Welsh International Rugby – John Billot (Ron Jones Publications)

The All Blacks in Wales – John Billot (Ron Jones Publications)

The Springboks in Wales – John Billot (Ron Jones Publications)

The Phoenix Book of International Rugby Records – John Griffiths (Phoenix House)

The Book of English International Rugby 1871–1982 – John Griffiths (Willow Books)

Rugby's Strangest Games – John Griffiths (Past Times)

The Complete Who's Who of International Rugby – Terry Godwin (Blandford Press)

The International Rugby Championship – Terry Godwin (Collins Willow)

The History of Glamorgan CCC –Andrew Hignell (Helm)

A 'Favourite' Game – Andrew Hignell (University of Wales Press)

Fields of Praise – David Smith and Gareth Williams (University of Wales Press)

Who's Who of Welsh International Rugby Players – Jenkins, Pierce and Auty (Bridge Books)

Rugby Recollections – WJT Collins (Johns)

Prince Gwyn – David Parry-Jones (Seren)

The Cardiff Rugby Football Club History and Statistics 1876–1906 – CS Arthur

Cardiff Rugby Club History and Statistics 1876–1975 – DE Davies (Starling Press)

Newport Rugby Greats – Alan Roderick (Handpost Books)

Newport Athletic Club 1875–1925

IRB World Rugby Yearbook 2007 (Vision Sports Publishing)

Welsh International Matches 1881–2000 – Howard Evans (Mainstream)

Welsh Brewers Rugby Annual for Wales 1969–70 to 1997–98

Worthington Rugby Annual for Wales 1998–99

Buy As You View Rugby Annual for Wales 1999–2000 to 2004–05

Rugby Annual for Wales 2005–06 and 2006–07

— WALES' RESULTS 1871–2007 —

A complete list of Wales' 576 official test match results, up to 18th August 2007.

Wales' record in those matches is won 298, drawn 27, lost 251, they have scored 8,991 points from 1,284 tries, 711 conversions, 808 penalty goals, 122 drop goals and 3 goals from a mark, and conceded 7,998 points.

Key

RWC Rugby World Cup
WCQ World Cup Qualifier
4NC Four Nations Championship
5NC Five Nations Championship
6NC Six Nations Championship
(1) First Test
(2) Second Test
(qf) Quarter-final
(sf) Semi-final
(f) Final
(3/4) Third and Fourth place play-off

No	Date	Opponents	Trn	Venue	Result
1	19 Feb 1881	England		Blackheath	Lost 0–7g,1dg,6t
2	28 Jan 1882	Ireland		Lansdowne Road	Won 2g,2t-0
3	16 Dec 1882	England	4NC	Swansea	Lost 0–2g,4t
4	8 Jan 1883	Scotland	4NC	Raeburn Place	Lost 1g-3g
5	5 Jan 1884	England	4NC	Leeds	Lost 1g-1g,2t
6	12 Jan 1884	Scotland	4NC	Newport	Lost 0–1dg,1t
7	12 Apr 1884	Ireland	4NC	Arms Park, Cardiff	Won 1dg,2t-0
8	3 Jan 1885	England	4NC	Swansea	Lost 1g,1t-1g,4t
9	10 Jan 1885	Scotland	4NC	Glasgow	Drew 0–0
10	2 Jan 1886	England	4NC	Blackheath	Lost 1g-2t
11	9 Jan 1886	Scotland	4NC	Arms Park, Cardiff	Lost 0–2g,1t
12	8 Jan 1887	England	4NC	Llanelli	Drew 0–0
13	26 Feb 1887	Scotland	4NC	Raeburn Place	Lost 0–4g,8t
14	12 Mar 1887	Ireland	4NC	Birkenhead Park	Won 1dg,1t-3t
15	4 Feb 1888	Scotland	4NC	Newport	Won 1t-0
16	3 Mar 1888	Ireland	4NC	Lansdowne Road	Lost 0–1g,1dg,1t
17	22 Dec 1888	New Zealand Natives		Swansea	Won 1g,2t-0
18	2 Feb 1889	Scotland	4NC	Raeburn Place	Lost 0–2t

19	2 Mar 1889	Ireland	4NC	Swansea	Lost 0–2t
20	1 Feb 1890	Scotland	4NC	Arms Park, Cardiff	Lost 2–8
21	15 Feb 1890	England	4NC	Dewsbury	Won 1–0
22	1 Mar 1890	Ireland	4NC	Lansdowne Road	Drew 3–3
23	3 Jan 1891	England	4NC	Newport	Lost 3–7
24	7 Feb 1891	Scotland	4NC	Raeburn Place	Lost 0–15
25	7 Mar 1891	Ireland	4NC	Llanelli	Won 6–4
26	2 Jan 1892	England	4NC	Blackheath	Lost 0–17
27	6 Feb 1892	Scotland	4NC	Swansea	Lost 2–7
28	5 Mar 1892	Ireland	4NC	Lansdowne Road	Lost 0–9
29	7 Jan 1893	England	4NC	Arms Park, Cardiff	Won 12–11
30	4 Feb 1893	Scotland	4NC	Raeburn Place	Won 9–0
31	11 Mar 1893	Ireland	4NC	Llanelli	Won 2–0
32	6 Jan 1894	England	4NC	Birkenhead Park	Lost 3–24
33	3 Feb 1894	Scotland	4NC	Newport	Won 7–0
34	10 Mar 1894	Ireland	4NC	Belfast	Lost 0–3
35	5 Jan 1895	England	4NC	Swansea	Lost 6–14
36	26 Jan 1895	Scotland	4NC	Raeburn Place	Lost 4–5
37	16 Mar 1895	Ireland	4NC	Arms Park, Cardiff	Won 5–3
38	4 Jan 1896	England	4NC	Blackheath	Lost 0–25
39	25 Jan 1896	Scotland	4NC	Arms Park, Cardiff	Won 6–0
40	14 Mar 1896	Ireland	4NC	Lansdowne Road	Lost 4–8
41	9 Jan 1897	England	4NC	Newport	Won 11–0
42	19 Mar 1898	Ireland	4NC	Limerick	Won 11–3
43	2 Apr 1898	England	4NC	Blackheath	Lost 7–14
44	7 Jan 1899	England	4NC	Swansea	Won 26–3
45	4 Mar 1899	Scotland	4NC	Inverleith	Lost 10–21
46	18 Mar 1899	Ireland	4NC	Arms Park, Cardiff	Lost 0–3
47	6 Jan 1900	England	4NC	Gloucester	Won 13–3
48	27 Jan 1900	Scotland	4NC	Swansea	Won 12–3
49	17 Mar 1900	Ireland	4NC	Belfast	Won 3–0
50	5 Jan 1901	England	4NC	Arms Park, Cardiff	Won 13–0
51	9 Feb 1901	Scotland	4NC	Inverleith	Lost 8–18
52	16 Mar 1901	Ireland	4NC	Swansea	Won 10–9
53	11 Jan 1902	England	4NC	Blackheath	Won 9–8
54	1 Feb 1902	Scotland	4NC	Arms Park, Cardiff	Won 14–5
55	8 Mar 1902	Ireland	4NC	Lansdowne Road	Won 15–0
56	10 Jan 1903	England	4NC	Swansea	Won 21–5
57	7 Feb 1903	Scotland	4NC	Inverleith	Lost 0–6
58	14 Mar 1903	Ireland	4NC	Arms Park, Cardiff	Won 18–0

59	9 Jan 1904	England	4NC	Leicester	Drew 14–14
60	6 Feb 1904	Scotland	4NC	Swansea	Won 21–3
61	12 Mar 1904	Ireland	4NC	Belfast	Lost 12–14
62	14 Jan 1905	England	4NC	Arms Park, Cardiff	Won 25–0
63	4 Feb 1905	Scotland	4NC	Inverleith	Won 6–3
64	11 Mar 1905	Ireland	4NC	Swansea	Won 10–3
65	16 Dec 1905	New Zealand		Arms Park, Cardiff	Won 3–0
66	13 Jan 1906	England	4NC	Richmond	Won 16–3
67	3 Feb 1906	Scotland	4NC	Arms Park, Cardiff	Won 9–3
68	10 Mar 1906	Ireland	4NC	Belfast	Lost 6–11
69	1 Dec 1906	South Africa		Swansea	Lost 0–11
70	12 Jan 1907	England	4NC	Swansea	Won 22–0
71	2 Feb 1907	Scotland	4NC	Inverleith	Lost 3–6
72	9 Mar 1907	Ireland	4NC	Arms Park, Cardiff	Won 29–0
73	18 Jan 1908	England	4NC	Bristol	Won 28–18
74	1 Feb 1908	Scotland	4NC	Swansea	Won 6–5
75	2 Mar 1908	France		Arms Park, Cardiff	Won 36–4
76	14 Mar 1908	Ireland	4NC	Belfast	Won 11–5
77	12 Dec 1908	Australia		Arms Park, Cardiff	Won 9–6
78	16 Jan 1909	England	4NC	Arms Park, Cardiff	Won 8–0
79	6 Feb 1909	Scotland	4NC	Inverleith	Won 5–3
80	23 Feb 1909	France		Stade Colombes	Won 47–5
81	13 Mar 1909	Ireland	4NC	Swansea	Won 18–5
82	1 Jan 1910	France	5NC	Swansea	Won 49–14
83	15 Jan 1910	England	5NC	Twickenham	Lost 6–11
84	5 Feb 1910	Scotland	5NC	Arms Park, Cardiff	Won 14–0
85	12 Mar 1910	Ireland	5NC	Lansdowne Road	Won 19–3
86	21 Jan 1911	England	5NC	Swansea	Won 15–11
87	4 Feb 1911	Scotland	5NC	Inverleith	Won 32–10
88	28 Feb 1911	France	5NC	Parc des Princes	Won 15–0
89	11 Mar 1911	Ireland	5NC	Arms Park, Cardiff	Won 16–0
90	20 Jan 1912	England	5NC	Twickenham	Lost 0–8
91	3 Feb 1912	Scotland	5NC	Swansea	Won 21–6
92	9 Mar 1912	Ireland	5NC	Belfast	Lost 5–12
93	25 Mar 1912	France	5NC	Newport	Won 14–8
94	14 Dec 1912	South Africa		Arms Park, Cardiff	Lost 0–3
95	18 Jan 1913	England	5NC	Arms Park, Cardiff	Lost 0–12

96	1 Feb 1913	Scotland	5NC	Inverleith	Won 8–0
97	27 Feb 1913	France	5NC	Parc des Princes	Won 11–8
98	8 Mar 1913	Ireland	5NC	Swansea	Won 16–13
99	17 Jan 1914	England	5NC	Twickenham	Lost 9–10
100	7 Feb 1914	Scotland	5NC	Arms Park, Cardiff	Won 24–5
101	2 Mar 1914	France	5NC	Swansea	Won 31–0
102	14 Mar 1914	Ireland	5NC	Belfast	Won 11–3
103	21 Apr 1919	New Zealand Services		Swansea	Lost 3–6
104	17 Jan 1920	England	5NC	Swansea	Won 19–5
105	7 Feb 1920	Scotland	5NC	Inverleith	Lost 5–9
106	17 Feb 1920	France	5NC	Stade Colombes	Won 6–5
107	13 Mar 1920	Ireland	5NC	Arms Park, Cardiff	Won 28–4
108	15 Jan 1921	England	5NC	Twickenham	Lost 3–18
109	5 Feb 1921	Scotland	5NC	Swansea	Lost 8–14
110	26 Feb 1921	France	5NC	Arms Park, Cardiff	Won 12–4
111	12 Mar 1921	Ireland	5NC	Belfast	Won 6–0
112	21 Jan 1922	England	5NC	Arms Park, Cardiff	Won 28–6
113	4 Feb 1922	Scotland	5NC	Inverleith	Drew 9–9
114	11 Mar 1922	Ireland	5NC	Swansea	Won 11–5
115	23 Mar 1922	France	5NC	Stade Colombes	Won 11–3
116	20 Jan 1923	England	5NC	Twickenham	Lost 3–7
117	3 Feb 1923	Scotland	5NC	Arms Park, Cardiff	Lost 8–11
118	24 Feb 1923	France	5NC	Swansea	Won 16–8
119	10 Mar 1923	Ireland	5NC	Lansdowne Road	Lost 4–5
120	19 Jan 1924	England	5NC	Swansea	Lost 9–17
121	2 Feb 1924	Scotland	5NC	Inverleith	Lost 10–35
122	8 Mar 1924	Ireland	5NC	Arms Park, Cardiff	Lost 10–13
123	27 Mar 1924	France	5NC	Stade Colombes	Won 10–6
124	29 Nov 1924	New Zealand		Swansea	Lost 0–19
125	17 Jan 1925	England	5NC	Twickenham	Lost 6–12
126	7 Feb 1925	Scotland	5NC	Swansea	Lost 14–24
127	28 Feb 1925	France	5NC	Arms Park, Cardiff	Won 11–5
128	14 Mar 1925	Ireland	5NC	Belfast	Lost 3–19
129	16 Jan 1926	England	5NC	Arms Park, Cardiff	Drew 3–3
130	6 Feb 1926	Scotland	5NC	Murrayfield	Lost 5–8
131	13 Mar 1926	Ireland	5NC	Swansea	Won 11–8
132	5 Apr 1926	France	5NC	Stade Colombes	Won 7–5
133	15 Jan 1927	England	5NC	Twickenham	Lost 9–11

134	5 Feb 1927	Scotland	5NC	Arms Park, Cardiff	Lost 0–5
135	26 Feb 1927	France	5NC	Swansea	Won 25–7
136	12 Mar 1927	Ireland	5NC	Lansdowne Road	Lost 9–19
137	26 Nov 1927	New South Wales		Arms Park, Cardiff	Lost 8–18
138	21 Jan 1928	England	5NC	Swansea	Lost 8–10
139	4 Feb 1928	Scotland	5NC	Murrayfield	Won 13–0
140	10 Mar 1928	Ireland	5NC	Arms Park, Cardiff	Lost 10–13
141	9 Apr 1928	France	5NC	Stade Colombes	Lost 3–8
142	19 Jan 1929	England	5NC	Twickenham	Lost 3–8
143	2 Feb 1929	Scotland	5NC	Swansea	Won 14–7
144	23 Feb 1929	France	5NC	Arms Park, Cardiff	Won 8–3
145	9 Mar 1929	Ireland	5NC	Belfast	Drew 5–5
146	18 Jan 1930	England	5NC	Arms Park, Cardiff	Lost 3–11
147	1 Feb 1930	Scotland	5NC	Murrayfield	Lost 9–12
148	8 Mar 1930	Ireland	5NC	Swansea	Won 12–7
149	21 Apr 1930	France	5NC	Stade Colombes	Won 11–0
150	17 Jan 1931	England	5NC	Twickenham	Drew 11–11
151	7 Feb 1931	Scotland	5NC	Arms Park, Cardiff	Won 13–8
152	28 Feb 1931	France	5NC	Swansea	Won 35–3
153	14 Mar 1931	Ireland	5NC	Belfast	Won 15–3
154	5 Dec 1931	South Africa		Swansea	Lost 3–8
155	16 Jan 1932	England	4NC	Swansea	Won 12–5
156	6 Feb 1932	Scotland	4NC	Murrayfield	Won 6–0
157	12 Mar 1932	Ireland	4NC	Arms Park, Cardiff	Lost 10–12
158	21 Jan 1933	England	4NC	Twickenham	Won 7–3
159	4 Feb 1933	Scotland	4NC	Swansea	Lost 3–11
160	11 Mar 1933	Ireland	4NC	Belfast	Lost 5–10
161	20 Jan 1934	England	4NC	Arms Park, Cardiff	Lost 0–9
162	3 Feb 1934	Scotland	4NC	Murrayfield	Won 13–6
163	10 Mar 1934	Ireland	4NC	Swansea	Won 13–0
164	19 Jan 1935	England	4NC	Twickenham	Drew 3–3
165	2 Feb 1935	Scotland	4NC	Arms Park, Cardiff	Won 10–6
166	9 Mar 1935	Ireland	4NC	Belfast	Lost 3–9
167	21 Dec 1935	New Zealand		Arms Park, Cardiff	Won 13–12
168	18 Jan 1936	England	4NC	Swansea	Drew 0–0
169	1 Feb 1936	Scotland	4NC	Murrayfield	Won 13–3
170	14 Mar 1936	Ireland	4NC	Arms Park, Cardiff	Won 3–0
171	16 Jan 1937	England	4NC	Twickenham	Lost 3–4

172	6 Feb 1937	Scotland	4NC	Swansea	Lost 6–13
173	3 Apr 1937	Ireland	4NC	Belfast	Lost 3–5
174	15 Jan 1938	England	4NC	Arms Park, Cardiff	Won 14–8
175	5 Feb 1938	Scotland	4NC	Murrayfield	Lost 6–8
176	12 Mar 1938	Ireland	4NC	Swansea	Won 11–5
177	21 Jan 1939	England	4NC	Twickenham	Lost 0–3
178	4 Feb 1939	Scotland	4NC	Arms Park, Cardiff	Won 11–3
179	11 Mar 1939	Ireland	4NC	Belfast	Won 7–0
180	18 Jan 1947	England	5NC	Arms Park, Cardiff	Lost 6–9
181	1 Feb 1947	Scotland	5NC	Murrayfield	Won 22–8
182	22 Mar 1947	France	5NC	Stade Colombes	Won 3–0
183	29 Mar 1947	Ireland	5NC	Swansea	Won 6–0
184	20 Dec 1947	Australia		Arms Park, Cardiff	Won 6–0
185	17 Jan 1948	England	5NC	Twickenham	Drew 3–3
186	7 Feb 1948	Scotland	5NC	Arms Park, Cardiff	Won 14–0
187	21 Feb 1948	France	5NC	Swansea	Lost 3–11
188	13 Mar 1948	Ireland	5NC	Belfast	Lost 3–6
189	15 Jan 1949	England	5NC	Arms Park, Cardiff	Won 9–3
190	5 Feb 1949	Scotland	5NC	Murrayfield	Lost 5–6
191	12 Mar 1949	Ireland	5NC	Swansea	Lost 0–5
192	26 Mar 1949	France	5NC	Stade Colombes	Lost 3–5
193	21 Jan 1950	England	5NC	Twickenham	Won 11–5
194	4 Feb 1950	Scotland	5NC	Swansea	Won 12–0
195	11 Mar 1950	Ireland	5NC	Belfast	Won 6–3
196	25 Mar 1950	France	5NC	Arms Park, Cardiff	Won 21–0
197	20 Jan 1951	England	5NC	Swansea	Won 23–5
198	3 Feb 1951	Scotland	5NC	Murrayfield	Lost 0–19
199	10 Mar 1951	Ireland	5NC	Arms Park, Cardiff	Drew 3–3
200	7 Apr 1951	France	5NC	Stade Colombes	Lost 3–8
201	22 Dec 1951	South Africa		Arms Park, Cardiff	Lost 3–6
202	19 Jan 1952	England	5NC	Twickenham	Won 8–6
203	2 Feb 1952	Scotland	5NC	Arms Park, Cardiff	Won 11–0
204	8 Mar 1952	Ireland	5NC	Lansdowne Road	Won 14–3
205	22 Mar 1952	France	5NC	Swansea	Won 9–5
206	17 Jan 1953	England	5NC	Arms Park, Cardiff	Lost 3–8
207	7 Feb 1953	Scotland	5NC	Murrayfield	Won 12–0
208	14 Mar 1953	Ireland	5NC	Swansea	Won 5–3
209	28 Mar 1953	France	5NC	Stade Colombes	Won 6–3
210	19 Dec 1953	New Zealand		Arms Park, Cardiff	Won 13–8

211	16 Jan 1954	England	5NC	Twickenham	Lost 6–9
212	13 Mar 1954	Ireland	5NC	Lansdowne Road	Won 12–9
213	27 Mar 1954	France	5NC	Arms Park, Cardiff	Won 19–13
214	10 Apr 1954	Scotland	5NC	Swansea	Won 15–3
215	22 Jan 1955	England	5NC	Arms Park, Cardiff	Won 3–0
216	5 Feb 1955	Scotland	5NC	Murrayfield	Lost 8–14
217	12 Mar 1955	Ireland	5NC	Arms Park, Cardiff	Won 21–3
218	26 Mar 1955	France	5NC	Stade Colombes	Won 16–11
219	21 Jan 1956	England	5NC	Twickenham	Won 8–3
220	4 Feb 1956	Scotland	5NC	Arms Park, Cardiff	Won 9–3
221	10 Mar 1956	Ireland	5NC	Lansdowne Road	Lost 3–11
222	24 Mar 1956	France	5NC	Arms Park, Cardiff	Won 5–3
223	19 Jan 1957	England	5NC	Arms Park, Cardiff	Lost 0–3
224	2 Feb 1957	Scotland	5NC	Murrayfield	Lost 6–9
225	9 Mar 1957	Ireland	5NC	Arms Park, Cardiff	Won 6–5
226	23 Mar 1957	France	5NC	Stade Colombes	Won 19–13
227	4 Jan 1958	Australia		Arms Park, Cardiff	Won 9–3
228	18 Jan 1958	England	5NC	Twickenham	Drew 3–3
229	1 Feb 1958	Scotland	5NC	Arms Park, Cardiff	Won 8–3
230	15 Mar 1958	Ireland	5NC	Lansdowne Road	Won 9–6
231	29 Mar 1958	France	5NC	Arms Park, Cardiff	Lost 6–16
232	17 Jan 1959	England	5NC	Arms Park, Cardiff	Won 5–0
233	7 Feb 1959	Scotland	5NC	Murrayfield	Lost 5–6
234	14 Mar 1959	Ireland	5NC	Arms Park, Cardiff	Won 8–6
235	4 Apr 1959	France	5NC	Stade Colombes	Lost 3–11
236	16 Jan 1960	England	5NC	Twickenham	Lost 6–14
237	6 Feb 1960	Scotland	5NC	Arms Park, Cardiff	Won 8–0
238	12 Mar 1960	Ireland	5NC	Lansdowne Road	Won 10–9
239	26 Mar 1960	France	5NC	Arms Park, Cardiff	Lost 8–16
240	3 Dec 1960	South Africa		Arms Park, Cardiff	Lost 0–3
241	21 Jan 1961	England	5NC	Arms Park, Cardiff	Won 6–3
242	11 Feb 1961	Scotland	5NC	Murrayfield	Lost 0–3
243	11 Mar 1961	Ireland	5NC	Arms Park, Cardiff	Won 9–0
244	25 Mar 1961	France	5NC	Stade Colombes	Lost 6–8
245	20 Jan 1962	England	5NC	Twickenham	Drew 0–0
246	3 Feb 1962	Scotland	5NC	Arms Park, Cardiff	Lost 3–8
247	24 Mar 1962	France	5NC	Arms Park, Cardiff	Won 3–0
248	17 Nov 1962	Ireland	5NC	Lansdowne Road	Drew 3–3
249	19 Jan 1963	England	5NC	Arms Park, Cardiff	Lost 6–13

250	2 Feb 1963	Scotland	5NC	Murrayfield	Won 6–0
251	9 Mar 1963	Ireland	5NC	Arms Park, Cardiff	Lost 6–14
252	23 Mar 1963	France	5NC	Stade Colombes	Lost 3–5
253	21 Dec 1963	New Zealand		Arms Park, Cardiff	Lost 0–6
254	18 Jan 1964	England	5NC	Twickenham	Drew 6–6
255	1 Feb 1964	Scotland	5NC	Arms Park, Cardiff	Won 11–3
256	7 Mar 1964	Ireland	5NC	Lansdowne Road	Won 15–6
257	21 Mar 1964	France	5NC	Arms Park, Cardiff	Drew 11–11
258	23 May 1964	South Africa		Durban	Lost 3–24
259	16 Jan 1965	England	5NC	Arms Park, Cardiff	Won 14–3
260	6 Feb 1965	Scotland	5NC	Murrayfield	Won 14–12
261	13 Mar 1965	Ireland	5NC	Arms Park, Cardiff	Won 14–8
262	27 Mar 1965	France	5NC	Stade Colombes	Lost 13–22
263	15 Jan 1966	England	5NC	Twickenham	Won 11–6
264	5 Feb 1966	Scotland	5NC	Arms Park, Cardiff	Won 8–3
265	12 Mar 1966	Ireland	5NC	Lansdowne Road	Lost 6–9
266	26 Mar 1966	France	5NC	Arms Park, Cardiff	Won 9–8
267	3 Dec 1966	Australia		Arms Park, Cardiff	Lost 11–14
268	4 Feb 1967	Scotland	5NC	Murrayfield	Lost 5–11
269	11 Mar 1967	Ireland	5NC	Arms Park, Cardiff	Lost 0–3
270	1 Apr 1967	France	5NC	Stade Colombes	Lost 14–20
271	15 Apr 1967	England	5NC	Arms Park, Cardiff	Won 34–21
272	11 Nov 1967	New Zealand		Arms Park, Cardiff	Lost 6–13
273	20 Jan 1968	England	5NC	Twickenham	Drew 11–11
274	3 Feb 1968	Scotland	5NC	Arms Park, Cardiff	Won 5–0
275	9 Mar 1968	Ireland	5NC	Lansdowne Road	Lost 6–9
276	23 Mar 1968	France	5NC	Arms Park, Cardiff	Lost 9–14
277	1 Feb 1969	Scotland	5NC	Murrayfield	Won 17–3
278	8 Mar 1969	Ireland	5NC	Arms Park, Cardiff	Won 24–11
279	22 Mar 1969	France	5NC	Stade Colombes	Drew 8–8
280	12 Apr 1969	England	5NC	Arms Park, Cardiff	Won 30–9
281	31 May 1969	New Zealand (1)		Christchurch	Lost 0–19
282	14 Jun 1969	New Zealand (2)		Auckland	Lost 12–33
283	21 Jun 1969	Australia		Sydney Cricket Ground	Won 19–16
284	24 Jan 1970	South Africa		Arms Park, Cardiff	Drew 6–6

285	7 Feb 1970	Scotland	5NC	Arms Park, Cardiff	Won 18–9
286	28 Feb 1970	England	5NC	Twickenham	Won 17–13
287	14 Mar 1970	Ireland	5NC	Lansdowne Road	Lost 0–14
288	4 Apr 1970	France	5NC	Arms Park, Cardiff	Won 11–6
289	16 Jan 1971	England	5NC	Arms Park, Cardiff	Won 22–6
290	6 Feb 1971	Scotland	5NC	Murrayfield	Won 19–18
291	13 Mar 1971	Ireland	5NC	Arms Park, Cardiff	Won 23–9
292	27 Mar 1971	France	5NC	Stade Colombes	Won 9–5
293	15 Jan 1972	England	5NC	Twickenham	Won 12–3
294	5 Feb 1972	Scotland	5NC	Arms Park, Cardiff	Won 35–12
295	25 Mar 1972	France	5NC	Arms Park, Cardiff	Won 20–6
296	2 Dec 1972	New Zealand		Arms Park, Cardiff	Lost 16–19
297	20 Jan 1973	England	5NC	Arms Park, Cardiff	Won 25–9
298	3 Feb 1973	Scotland	5NC	Murrayfield	Lost 9–10
299	10 Mar 1973	Ireland	5NC	Arms Park, Cardiff	Won 16–12
300	24 Mar 1973	France	5NC	Parc des Princes	Lost 3–12
301	10 Nov 1973	Australia		Arms Park, Cardiff	Won 24–0
302	19 Jan 1974	Scotland	5NC	Arms Park, Cardiff	Won 6–0
303	2 Feb 1974	Ireland	5NC	Lansdowne Road	Drew 9–9
304	16 Feb 1974	France	5NC	Arms Park, Cardiff	Drew 16–16
305	16 Mar 1974	England	5NC	Twickenham	Lost 12–16
306	18 Jan 1975	France	5NC	Parc des Princes	Won 25–10
307	15 Feb 1975	England	5NC	Arms Park, Cardiff	Won 20–4
308	1 Mar 1975	Scotland	5NC	Murrayfield	Lost 10–12
309	15 Mar 1975	Ireland	5NC	Arms Park, Cardiff	Won 32–4
310	20 Dec 1975	Australia		Arms Park, Cardiff	Won 28–3
311	17 Jan 1976	England	5NC	Twickenham	Won 21–9
312	7 Feb 1976	Scotland	5NC	Arms Park, Cardiff	Won 28–6
313	21 Feb 1976	Ireland	5NC	Lansdowne Road	Won 34–9
314	6 Mar 1976	France	5NC	Arms Park, Cardiff	Won 19–13
315	15 Jan 1977	Ireland	5NC	Arms Park, Cardiff	Won 25–9
316	5 Feb 1977	France	5NC	Parc des Princes	Lost 9–16
317	5 Mar 1977	England	5NC	Arms Park, Cardiff	Won 14–9
318	19 Mar 1977	Scotland	5NC	Murrayfield	Won 18–9
319	4 Feb 1978	England	5NC	Twickenham	Won 9–6
320	18 Feb 1978	Scotland	5NC	Arms Park, Cardiff	Won 22–14
321	4 Mar 1978	Ireland	5NC	Lansdowne Road	Won 20–16
322	18 Mar 1978	France	5NC	Arms Park, Cardiff	Won 16–7
323	11 Jun 1978	Australia (1)		Brisbane	Lost 8–18

324	17 Jun 1978	Australia (2)		Sydney Cricket Ground	Lost 17–19
325	11 Nov 1978	New Zealand		Arms Park, Cardiff	Lost 12–13
326	20 Jan 1979	Scotland	5NC	Murrayfield	Won 19–13
327	3 Feb 1979	Ireland	5NC	Arms Park, Cardiff	Won 24–21
328	17 Feb 1979	France	5NC	Parc des Princes	Lost 13–14
329	17 Mar 1979	England	5NC	Arms Park, Cardiff	Won 27–3
330	19 Jan 1980	France	5NC	Arms Park, Cardiff	Won 18–9
331	16 Feb 1980	England	5NC	Twickenham	Lost 8–9
332	1 Mar 1980	Scotland	5NC	Arms Park, Cardiff	Won 17–6
333	15 Mar 1980	Ireland	5NC	Lansdowne Road	Lost 7–21
334	1 Nov 1980	New Zealand		Arms Park, Cardiff	Lost 3–23
335	17 Jan 1981	England	5NC	Arms Park, Cardiff	Won 21–19
336	7 Feb 1981	Scotland	5NC	Murrayfield	Lost 6–15
337	21 Feb 1981	Ireland	5NC	Arms Park, Cardiff	Won 9–8
338	7 Mar 1981	France	5NC	Parc des Princes	Lost 15–19
339	5 Dec 1981	Australia		Arms Park, Cardiff	Won 18–13
340	23 Jan 1982	Ireland	5NC	Lansdowne Road	Lost 12–20
341	6 Feb 1982	France	5NC	Arms Park, Cardiff	Won 22–12
342	6 Mar 1982	England	5NC	Twickenham	Lost 7–17
343	20 Mar 1982	Scotland	5NC	Arms Park, Cardiff	Lost 18–34
344	5 Feb 1983	England	5NC	Arms Park, Cardiff	Drew 13–13
345	19 Feb 1983	Scotland	5NC	Murrayfield	Won 19–15
346	5 Mar 1983	Ireland	5NC	Arms Park, Cardiff	Won 23–9
347	19 Mar 1983	France	5NC	Parc des Princes	Lost 9–16
348	12 Nov 1983	Romania		Bucharest	Lost 6–24
349	21 Jan 1984	Scotland	5NC	Arms Park, Cardiff	Lost 9–15
350	4 Feb 1984	Ireland	5NC	Lansdowne Road	Won 18–9
351	18 Feb 1984	France	5NC	Arms Park, Cardiff	Lost 16–21
352	17 Mar 1984	England	5NC	Twickenham	Won 24–15
353	24 Nov 1984	Australia		Arms Park, Cardiff	Lost 9–28
354	2 Mar 1985	Scotland	5NC	Murrayfield	Won 25–21
355	16 Mar 1985	Ireland	5NC	Arms Park, Cardiff	Lost 9–21
356	30 Mar 1985	France	5NC	Parc des Princes	Lost 3–14
357	20 Apr 1985	England	5NC	Arms Park, Cardiff	Won 24–15
358	9 Nov 1985	Fiji		Arms Park, Cardiff	Won 40–3
359	18 Jan 1986	England	5NC	Twickenham	Lost 18–21
360	1 Feb 1986	Scotland	5NC	Arms Park, Cardiff	Won 22–15

361	15 Feb 1986	Ireland	5NC	Lansdowne Road	Won 19–12
362	1 Mar 1986	France	5NC	Arms Park, Cardiff	Lost 15–23
363	31 May 1986	Fiji	Suva	Won 22–15	
364	12 Jun 1986	Tonga		Nuku A'lofa	Won 15–7
365	14 Jun 1986	W Samoa		Apia Park	Won 32–14
366	7 Feb 1987	France	5NC	Parc des Princes	Lost 9–16
367	7 Mar 1987	England	5NC	Arms Park, Cardiff	Won 19–12
368	21 Mar 1987	Scotland	5NC	Murrayfield	Lost 15–21
369	4 Apr 1987	Ireland	5NC	Arms Park, Cardiff	Lost 11–15
370	25 May 1987	Ireland	RWC	Wellington	Won 13–6
371	29 May 1987	Tonga	RWC	Palmerston North	Won 29–16
372	3 Jun 1987	Canada	RWC	Invercargill	Won 40–9
373	8 Jun 1987	England (qf)	RWC	Brisbane	Won 16–3
374	14 Jun 1987	New Zealand (sf)	RWC	Brisbane	Lost 6–49
375	18 Jun 1987	Australia (3/4)	RWC	Rotorua	Won 22–21
376	7 Nov 1987	United States		Arms Park, Cardiff	Won 46–0
377	6 Feb 1988	England	5NC	Twickenham	Won 11–3
378	20 Feb 1988	Scotland	5NC	Arms Park, Cardiff	Won 25–20
379	5 Mar 1988	Ireland	5NC	Lansdowne Road	Won 12–9
380	19 Mar 1988	France	5NC	Arms Park, Cardiff	Lost 9–10
381	28 May 1988	New Zealand (1)		Christchurch	Lost 3–52
382	11 Jun 1988	New Zealand (2)		Auckland	Lost 9–54
383	12 Nov 1988	W Samoa		Arms Park, Cardiff	Won 24–6
384	10 Dec 1988	Romania		Arms Park, Cardiff	Lost 9–15
385	21 Jan 1989	Scotland	5NC	Murrayfield	Lost 7–23
386	4 Feb 1989	Ireland	5NC	Arms Park, Cardiff	Lost 13–19
387	18 Feb 1989	France	5NC	Parc des Princes	Lost 12–31
388	18 Mar 1989	England	5NC	Arms Park, Cardiff	Won 12–9
389	4 Nov 1989	New Zealand		Arms Park, Cardiff	Lost 9–34
390	20 Jan 1990	France	5NC	Arms Park, Cardiff	Lost 19–29
391	17 Feb 1990	England	5NC	Twickenham	Lost 6–34
392	3 Mar 1990	Scotland	5NC	Arms Park, Cardiff	Lost 9–13
393	24 Mar 1990	Ireland	5NC	Lansdowne Road	Lost 8–14

394	2 Jun 1990	Namibia (1)		Windhoek	Won 18–9
395	9 Jun 1990	Namibia (2)		Windhoek	Won 34–30
396	6 Oct 1990	Barbarians		Arms Park, Cardiff	Lost 24–31
397	19 Jan 1991	England	5NC	Arms Park, Cardiff	Lost 6–25
398	2 Feb 1991	Scotland	5NC	Murrayfield	Lost 12–32
399	16 Feb 1991	Ireland	5NC	Arms Park, Cardiff	Drew 21–21
400	2 Mar 1991	France	5NC	Parc des Princes	Lost 3–36
401	22 Jul 1991	Australia		Brisbane	Lost 6–63
402	4 Sep 1991	France		Arms Park, Cardiff	Lost 9–22
403	6 Oct 1991	W Samoa	RWC	Arms Park, Cardiff	Lost 13–16
404	9 Oct 1991	Argentina	RWC	Arms Park, Cardiff	Won 16–7
405	12 Oct 1991	Australia	RWC	Arms Park, Cardiff	Lost 3–38
406	18 Jan 1992	Ireland	5NC	Lansdowne Road	Won 16–15
407	1 Feb 1992	France	5NC	Arms Park, Cardiff	Lost 9–12
408	7 Mar 1992	England	5NC	Twickenham	Lost 0–24
409	21 Mar 1992	Scotland	5NC	Arms Park, Cardiff	Won 15–12
410	21 Nov 1992	Australia		Arms Park, Cardiff	Lost 6–23
411	6 Feb 1993	England	5NC	Arms Park, Cardiff	Won 10–9
412	20 Feb 1993	Scotland	5NC	Murrayfield	Lost 0–20
413	6 Mar 1993	Ireland	5NC	Arms Park, Cardiff	Lost 14–19
414	20 Mar 1993	France	5NC	Parc des Princes	Lost 10–26
415	22 May 1993	Zimbabwe (1)		Bulawayo	Won 35–14
416	29 May 1993	Zimbabwe (2)		Harare	Won 42–13
417	5 Jun 1993	Namibia		Windhoek	Won 38–23
418	16 Oct 1993	Japan		Arms Park, Cardiff	Won 55–5
419	10 Nov 1993	Canada		Arms Park, Cardiff	Lost 24–26
420	15 Jan 1994	Scotland	5NC	Arms Park, Cardiff	Won 29–6
421	5 Feb 1994	Ireland	5NC	Lansdowne Road	Won 17–15
422	19 Feb 1994	France	5NC	Arms Park, Cardiff	Won 24–15
423	19 Mar 1994	England	5NC	Twickenham	Lost 8–15
424	18 May 1994	Portugal	WCQ	Lisbon	Won 102–11
425	21 May 1994	Spain	WCQ	Madrid	Won 54–0
426	11 Jun 1994	Canada		Markham	Won 33–15
427	18 Jun 1994	Fiji		Suva	Won 23–8
428	22 Jun 1994	Tonga		Nuku A'lofa	Won 18–9
429	25 Jun 1994	W Samoa		Moamoa	Lost 9–34
430	17 Sep 1994	Romania	WCQ	Bucharest	Won 16–9
431	12 Oct 1994	Italy	WCQ	Arms Park, Cardiff	Won 29–19
432	26 Nov 1994	South	Africa	Arms Park, Cardiff	Lost 12–20
433	21 Jan 1995	France	5NC	Parc des Princes	Lost 9–21

434	18 Feb 1995	England	5NC	Arms Park, Cardiff	Lost 9–23
435	4 Mar 1995	Scotland	5NC	Murrayfield	Lost 13–26
436	18 Mar 1995	Ireland	5NC	Arms Park, Cardiff	Lost 12–16
437	27 May 1995	Japan	RWC	Bloemfontein	Won 57–10
438	31 May 1995	New Zealand	RWC	Johannesburg	Lost 9–34
439	4 Jun 1995	Ireland	RWC	Johannesburg	Lost 23–24
440	2 Sep 1995	South Africa		Johannesburg	Lost 11–40
441	11 Nov 1995	Fiji		Arms Park, Cardiff	Won 19–15
442	16 Jan 1996	Italy		Arms Park, Cardiff	Won 31–26
443	3 Feb 1996	England	5NC	Twickenham	Lost 15–21
444	17 Feb 1996	Scotland	5NC	Arms Park, Cardiff	Lost 14–16
445	2 Mar 1996	Ireland	5NC	Lansdowne Road	Lost 17–30
446	16 Mar 1996	France	5NC	Arms Park, Cardiff	Won 16–15
447	9 Jun 1996	Australia (1)		Brisbane	Lost 25–56
448	22 Jun 1996	Australia (2)		Sydney Football Stadium	Lost 3–42
449	24 Aug 1996	Barbarians		Arms Park, Cardiff	Won 31–10
450	25 Sep 1996	France		Arms Park, Cardiff	Lost 33–40
451	5 Oct 1996	Italy		Rome	Won 31–22
452	1 Dec 1996	Australia		Arms Park, Cardiff	Lost 19–28
453	15 Dec 1996	South Africa		Arms Park, Cardiff	Lost 20–37
454	11 Jan 1997	United States		Arms Park, Cardiff	Won 34–14
455	18 Jan 1997	Scotland	5NC	Murrayfield	Won 34–19
456	1 Feb 1997	Ireland	5NC	Arms Park, Cardiff	Lost 25–26
457	15 Feb 1997	France	5NC	Parc des Princes	Lost 22–27
458	15 Mar 1997	England	5NC	Arms Park, Cardiff	Lost 13–34
459	5 Jul 1997	United States (1)		Wilmington	Won 30–20
460	12 Jul 1997	United States (2)		San Francisco	Won 28–23
461	19 Jul 1997	Canada		Markham	Won 28–25
462	30 Aug 1997	Romania		Wrexham	Won 70–21
463	16 Nov 1997	Tonga		Swansea	Won 46–12
464	29 Nov 1997	New Zealand		Wembley	Lost 7–42
465	7 Feb 1998	Italy		Llanelli	Won 23–20

466	21 Feb 1998	England	5NC	Twickenham	Lost 26–60
467	7 Mar 1998	Scotland	5NC	Wembley	Won 19–13
468	21 Mar 1998	Ireland	5NC	Lansdowne Road	Won 30–21
469	5 Apr 1998	France	5NC	Wembley	Lost 0–51
470	6 Jun 1998	Zimbabwe		Harare	Won 49–11
471	27 Jun 1998	South Africa		Pretoria	Lost 13–96
472	14 Nov 1998	South Africa		Wembley	Lost 20–28
473	21 Nov 1998	Argentina		Llanelli	Won 43–30
474	6 Feb 1999	Scotland	5NC	Murrayfield	Lost 20–33
475	20 Feb 1999	Ireland	5NC	Wembley	Lost 23–29
476	6 Mar 1999	France	5NC	Stade de France	Won 34–33
477	20 Mar 1999	Italy		Treviso	Won 60–21
478	11 Apr 1999	England	5NC	Wembley	Won 32–31
479	5 Jun 1999	Argentina (1)		Buenos Aires	Won 36–26
480	12 Jun 1999	Argentina (2)		Buenos Aires	Won 23–16
481	26 Jun 1999	South Africa		Millennium Stadium	Won 29–19
482	21 Aug 1999	Canada		Millennium Stadium	Won 33–19
483	28 Aug 1999	France		Millennium Stadium	Won 34–23
484	1 Oct 1999	Argentina	RWC	Millennium Stadium	Won 23–18
485	9 Oct 1999	Japan	RWC	Millennium Stadium	Won 64–15
486	14 Oct 1999	Samoa	RWC	Millennium Stadium	Lost 31–38
487	23 Oct 1999	Australia	RWC	Millennium Stadium	Lost 9–24
488	5 Feb 2000	France	6NC	Millennium Stadium	Lost 3–36
489	19 Feb 2000	Italy	6NC	Millennium Stadium	Won 47–16
490	4 Mar 2000	England	6NC	Twickenham	Lost 12–46
491	18 Mar 2000	Scotland	6NC	Millennium Stadium	Won 26–18
492	1 Apr 2000	Ireland	6NC	Lansdowne Road	Won 23–19
493	11 Nov 2000	Samoa		Millennium Stadium	Won 50–6
494	18 Nov 2000	United States		Millennium Stadium	Won 42–11
495	26 Nov 2000	South Africa		Millennium Stadium	Lost 13–23
496	3 Feb 2001	England	6NC	Millennium Stadium	Lost 15–44
497	17 Feb 2001	Scotland	6NC	Murrayfield	Drew 28–28
498	17 Mar 2001	France	6NC	Stade de France	Won 43–35
499	8 Apr 2001	Italy	6NC	Rome	Won 33–23
500	10 Jun 2001	Japan (1)		Osaka	Won 64–10

501	17 Jun 2001	Japan (2)		Tokyo	Won 53–30
502	19 Sep 2001	Romania		Millennium Stadium	Won 81–9
503	13 Oct 2001	Ireland	6NC	Millennium Stadium	Lost 6–36
504	10 Nov 2001	Argentina		Millennium Stadium	Lost 16–30
505	17 Nov 2001	Tonga		Millennium Stadium	Won 51–7
506	25 Nov 2001	Australia		Millennium Stadium	Lost 13–21
507	3 Feb 2002	Ireland	6NC	Lansdowne Road	Lost 10–54
508	16 Feb 2002	France	6NC	Millennium Stadium	Lost 33–37
509	2 Mar 2002	Italy	6NC	Millennium Stadium	Won 44–20
510	23 Mar 2002	England	6NC	Twickenham	Lost 10–50
511	6 Apr 2002	Scotland	6NC	Millennium Stadium	Lost 22–27
512	8 Jun 2002	South Africa (1)		Bloemfontein	Lost 19–34
513	15 Jun 2002	South Africa (2)		Cape Town	Lost 8–19
514	1 Nov 2002	Romania		Wrexham	Won 40–3
515	9 Nov 2002	Fiji		Millennium Stadium	Won 58–14
516	16 Nov 2002	Canada		Millennium Stadium	Won 32–21
517	23 Nov 2002	New Zealand		Millennium Stadium	Lost 17–43
518	15 Feb 2003	Italy	6NC	Rome	Lost 22–30
519	22 Feb 2003	England	6NC	Millennium Stadium	Lost 9–26
520	8 Mar 2003	Scotland	6NC	Murrayfield	Lost 22–30
521	22 Mar 2003	Ireland	6NC	Millennium Stadium	Lost 24–25
522	29 Mar 2003	France	6NC	Stade de France	Lost 5–33
523	14 Jun 2003	Australia		Sydney	Lost 10–30
524	21 Jun 2003	New Zealand		Hamilton	Lost 3–55
525	16 Aug 2003	Ireland		Lansdowne Road	Lost 12–35
526	23 Aug 2003	England		Millennium Stadium	Lost 9–43
527	27 Aug 2003	Romania		Wrexham	Won 54–8
528	30 Aug 2003	Scotland		Millennium Stadium	Won 23–9
529	12 Oct 2003	Canada	RWC	Melbourne	Won 41–10
530	19 Oct 2003	Tonga	RWC	Canberra	Won 27–20
531	25 Oct 2003	Italy	RWC	Canberra	Won 27–15
532	2 Nov 2003	New Zealand	RWC	Sydney	Lost 37–53
533	9 Nov 2003	England (qf)	RWC	Brisbane	Lost 17–28
534	14 Feb 2004	Scotland	6NC	Millennium Stadium	Won 23–10

535	22 Feb 2004	Ireland	6NC	Lansdowne Road	Lost 15–36
536	7 Mar 2004	France	6NC	Millennium Stadium	Lost 22–29
537	20 Mar 2004	England	6NC	Twickenham	Lost 21–31
538	27 Mar 2004	Italy	6NC	Millennium Stadium	Won 44–10
539	12 Jun 2004	Argentina	(1)	Tucuman	Lost 44–50
540	19 Jun 2004	Argentina	(2)	Buenos Aires	Won 35–20
541	26 Jun 2004	South Africa		Pretoria	Lost 18–53
542	6 Nov 2004	South Africa		Millennium Stadium	Lost 36–38
543	12 Nov 2004	Romania		Millennium Stadium	Won 66–7
544	20 Nov 2004	New Zealand		Millennium Stadium	Lost 25–26
545	26 Nov 2004	Japan		Millennium Stadium	Won 98–0
546	5 Feb 2005	England	6NC	Millennium Stadium	Won 11–9
547	12 Feb 2005	Italy	6NC	Rome	Won 38–8
548	26 Feb 2005	France	6NC	Stade de France	Won 24–18
549	13 Mar 2005	Scotland	6NC	Murrayfield	Won 46–22
550	19 Mar 2005	Ireland	6NC	Millennium Stadium	Won 32–20
551	4 Jun 2005	United States		Hartford	Won 77–3
552	11 Jun 2005	Canada		Toronto	Won 60–3
553	5 Nov 2005	New Zealand		Millennium Stadium	Lost 3–41
554	11 Nov 2005	Fiji		Millennium Stadium	Won 11–10
555	19 Nov 2005	South Africa		Millennium Stadium	Lost 16–33
556	26 Nov 2005	Australia		Millennium Stadium	Won 24–22
557	4 Feb 2006	England	6NC	Twickenham	Lost 13–47
558	12 Feb 2006	Scotland	6NC	Millennium Stadium	Won 28–18
559	26 Feb 2006	Ireland	6NC	Lansdowne Road	Lost 5–31
560	11 Mar 2006	Italy	6NC	Millennium Stadium	Drew 18–18
561	18 Mar 2006	France	6NC	Millennium Stadium	Lost 16–21
562	11 Jun 2006	Argentina	(1)	Puerto Madryn	Lost 25–27
563	17 Jun 2006	Argentina	(2)	Buenos Aires	Lost 27–45
564	4 Nov 2006	Australia		Millennium Stadium	Drew 29–29
565	11 Nov 2006	Pacific Islanders		Millennium Stadium	Won 38–20
566	17 Nov 2006	Canada		Millennium Stadium	Won 61–26
567	25 Nov 2006	New Zealand		Millennium Stadium	Lost 10–45

568	4 Feb 2007	Ireland	6NC	Millennium Stadium	Lost 9–19
569	10 Feb 2007	Scotland	6NC	Murrayfield	Lost 9–21
570	24 Feb 2007	France	6NC	Stade de France	Lost 21–32
571	10 Mar 2007	Italy	6NC	Rome	Lost 20–23
572	17 Mar 2007	England	6NC	Millennium Stadium	Won 27–18
573	26 May 2007	Australia (1)		Sydney	Lost 23–29
574	2 Jun 2007	Australia (2)		Brisbane	Lost 0–31
575	4 Aug 2007	England		Twickenham	Lost 5–62
576	18 Aug 2007	Argentina		Millennium Stadium	Won 27–20
577	26 Aug 2007	France		Millennium Stadium	
578	9 Sep 2007	Canada	RWC	Nantes	
579	15 Sep 2007	Australia	RWC	Millennium Stadium	
580	20 Sep 2007	Japan	RWC	Millennium Stadium	
581	29 Sep 2007	Fiji	RWC	Nantes	

ICH DIEN